ACCOUNTING WORKSHEETS
A & B Problems Chapters 1 to 14

ACCOUNTING PRINCIPLES

Third Edition

Jack L. Smith, Ph.D., C.P.A.
School of Accountancy
University of South Florida

Robert M. Keith, Ph.D., C.P.A.
School of Accountancy
University of South Florida

William L. Stephens, D.B.A., C.P.A.
School of Accountancy
University of South Florida

McGraw-Hill Book Company
New York St. Louis San Francisco Auckland Bogotá Caracas
Colorado Springs Hamburg Lisbon London Madrid Mexico Milan
Montreal New Delhi Oklahoma City Panama Paris San Juan
São Paulo Singapore Sydney Tokyo Toronto

STUDY GUIDE
Available with Smith, Keith, and Stephens: *Accounting Principles,* Third Edition, is a student guide, written by Joe D. Icerman and Paul F. Williams, to assist you in mastering the concepts and calculations in the text. The *Study Guide* contains objectives, highlights, and self-testing questions and exercises for each chapter in the text. Answers are included at the back of the *Study Guide*. Check with your bookstore.

NOTE TO STUDENT
The worksheets in this book cover text Chapters 1 to 14. They are arranged in the following order: (1) worksheets for all A problems; (2) worksheets for all B problems; (3) foldout worksheets for the A problems; (4) foldout worksheets for the B problems.

3 4 5 6 7 8 9 0 SEM SEM 9 0 9 8 7 6 5 4 3 2 1

PROBLEM **A2-1**

NAME
SECTION
DATE

Robert Walton Arctic Exploring Service

1. **ROBERT WALTON ARCTIC EXPLORING SERVICE**
Income Statement
Month Ended January 31, 1990

Revenue:		
Expenses:		
Net Income		

2. **ROBERT WALTON ARCTIC EXPLORING SERVICE**
Statement of Owner's Equity
Month Ended January 31, 1990

PROBLEM **A2-3**

Waldman's Key Shoppe

NAME

SECTION

DATE

1.

WALDMAN'S KEY SHOPPE
Financial Transaction Worksheet
Month of February, 1990

Transaction	Cash	Accounts Receivable	Supplies on Hand	Equipment	Accounts Payable	Waldman, Capital	Owner's Equity Explanation
Start							
a.							
b.							
c.							
d.							
e.							
f.							
g.							
h.							
i.							
j.							
k.							

2.

Revenue

Expenses

Net Income

PROBLEM **A2-4**

Saville Delivery Service

NAME
SECTION
DATE

1.

SAVILLE DELIVERY SERVICE
Financial Transaction Worksheet
Month of October, 1990

Trans-action	Cash	Accounts Receivable	Office Supplies on Hand	Delivery Truck	Notes Payable	Accounts Payable	Saville, Capital	Owner's Equity Explanation
Start								
a.								
b.								
c.								
d.								
e.								
f.								
g.								
h.								
i.								
j.								
k.								

PROBLEM **A2-4**

Saville Delivery Service *(concluded)*

2.a.

SAVILLE DELIVERY SERVICE
Income Statement
For the Month Ended October 31, 1990

Revenue:		
Expenses:		
Net Income		

2.b.

SAVILLE DELIVERY SERVICE
Statement of Owner's Equity
Month Ended October 31, 1990

2.c.

SAVILLE DELIVERY SERVICE
Balance Sheet
October 31, 1990

Assets		**Liabilities & Owner's Equity**	
		Liabilities:	
		Owner's Equity:	
		Total Liabilities	
Total Assets		and Owner's Equity	

PROBLEM **A2-5** Worksheet for parts 1 and 2 of this problem is at the back of this book.

NAME
SECTION
DATE

Beaufort Nursing Home *(concluded)*

3.a.

BEAUFORT NURSING HOME
Income Statement
Month Ended January 31, 1990

Revenue:

Expenses:

Net Income

3.b.

BEAUFORT NURSING HOME
Statement of Owner's Equity
Month Ended January 31, 1990

BEAUFORT NURSING HOME
Balance Sheet
January 31, 1990

Assets		Liabilities & Owner's Equity	
		Liabilities:	
		Owner's Equity:	
Total Assets		Total Liabilities and Owner's Equity	

PROBLEM **A3-3**

The Redruth Company

NAME
SECTION
DATE

Date		General Journal Account Titles and Explanation	Post. Ref.	Debit	Credit
1990					
Nov.	1				

Accounts Receivable

Accounts Payable

Cash

PROBLEM **A3-4**

NAME
SECTION
DATE

Hawkins Child Safe Day Care Center

1.	General Journal			
		Post.		
Date	Account Titles and Explanation	Ref.	Debit	Credit
1990				
May				

PROBLEM **A3-4**

Hawkins Child Safe Day Care Center *(continued)*

	General Journal			
		Post.		
Date	Account Titles and Explanation	Ref.	Debit	Credit
1990				
May				

PROBLEM **A3-4**

NAME

SECTION

DATE

Hawkins Child Safe Day Care Center *(continued)*

General Ledger

Date	Cash Explanation	Post. Ref.	Debit	Credit	Acct. No. 110 Balance
1990					
May					

Date	Accounts Receivable Explanation	Post. Ref.	Debit	Credit	Acct. No. 120 Balance
1990					
May					

Date	Playground Supplies on Hand Explanation	Post. Ref.	Debit	Credit	Acct. No. 130 Balance
1990					
May					

Date	Land Explanation	Post. Ref.	Debit	Credit	Acct. No. 140 Balance
1990					
May					

Date	Building Explanation	Post. Ref.	Debit	Credit	Acct. No. 150 Balance
1990					
May					

PROBLEM **A3-4**

Hawkins Child Safe Day Care Center *(continued)*

Date		Playground Equipment Explanation	Post. Ref.	Debit	Credit	Acct. No. 160 Balance
1990						
May						

Date		Accounts Payable Explanation	Post. Ref.	Debit	Credit	Acct. No. 210 Balance
1990						
May						

Date		Mortgage Payable Explanation	Post. Ref.	Debit	Credit	Acct. No. 220 Balance
1990						
May						

Date		Hawkins, Capital Explanation	Post. Ref.	Debit	Credit	Acct. No. 310 Balance
1990						
May						

Date		Hawkins, Withdrawals Explanation	Post. Ref.	Debit	Credit	Acct. No. 320 Balance
1990						
May						

Date		Day Care Fees Earned Explanation	Post. Ref.	Debit	Credit	Acct. No. 410 Balance
1990						
May						

PROBLEM **A3-4**

NAME
SECTION
DATE

Hawkins Child Safe Day Care Center *(continued)*

Date		Salary Expense Explanation	Post. Ref.	Debit	Credit	Acct. No. 510 Balance
1990						
May						

Date		Insurance Expense Explanation	Post. Ref.	Debit	Credit	Acct. No. 520 Balance
1990						
May						

Date		Advertising Expense Explanation	Post. Ref.	Debit	Credit	Acct. No. 530 Balance
1990						
May						

Date		Repairs Expense Explanation	Post. Ref.	Debit	Credit	Acct. No. 540 Balance
1990						
May						

Date		Utilities Expense Explanation	Post. Ref.	Debit	Credit	Acct. No. 550 Balance
1990						
May						

Date		Miscellaneous Expense Explanation	Post. Ref.	Debit	Credit	Acct. No. 560 Balance
1990						
May						

PROBLEM **A3-4**

Hawkins Child Safe Day Care Center *(continued)*

3.

HAWKINS CHILD SAFE DAY CARE CENTER
Trial Balance
May 31, 1990

4.

HAWKINS CHILD SAFE DAY CARE CENTER
Income Statement
Month Ended May 31, 1990

HAWKINS CHILD SAFE DAY CARE CENTER
Statement of Changes in Owner's Equity
Month Ended May 31, 1990

PROBLEM **A3-4**

NAME
SECTION
DATE

Hawkins Child Safe Day Care Center *(concluded)*

HAWKINS CHILD SAFE DAY CARE CENTER			
Balance Sheet			
May 31, 1990			
Assets		**Liabilities & Owner's Equity**	

PROBLEM **A3-5**

Smollett Ships

NAME

SECTION

DATE

2.	General Journal			
		Post.		
Date	Account Titles and Explanation	Ref.	Debit	Credit
1990				
Sept.				

PROBLEM **A3-5**

Smollett Ships *(continued)*

Date		General Journal Account Titles and Explanation	Post. Ref.	Debit	Credit
1990					
Sept.					

PROBLEM **A3-5**

NAME

SECTION

DATE

Smollett Ships *(continued)*

General Ledger

1. and 3.

Date		Cash Explanation	Post. Ref.	Debit	Credit	Acct. No. 110 Balance
1990						
Sept.						

Date		Accounts Receivable Explanation	Post. Ref.	Debit	Credit	Acct. No. 120 Balance
1990						
Sept.						

Date		Prepaid Insurance Explanation	Post. Ref.	Debit	Credit	Acct. No. 130 Balance
1990						
Sept.						

Date		Ship Supplies on Hand Explanation	Post. Ref.	Debit	Credit	Acct. No. 140 Balance
1990						
Sept.						

PROBLEM **A3-5**

Smollett Ships *(continued)*

Date	Ship Equipment Explanation	Post. Ref.	Debit	Credit	Acct. No. 150 Balance
1990					
Sept.					

Date	Ships Explanation	Post. Ref.	Debit	Credit	Acct. No. 160 Balance
1990					
Sept.					

Date	Notes Payable Explanation	Post. Ref.	Debit	Credit	Acct. No. 210 Balance
1990					
Sept.					

Date	Accounts Payable Explanation	Post. Ref.	Debit	Credit	Acct. No. 220 Balance
1990					
Sept.					

Date	Smollett, Capital Explanation	Post. Ref.	Debit	Credit	Acct. No. 310 Balance
1990					
Sept.					

PROBLEM **A3-5**

NAME
SECTION
DATE

Smollett Ships *(continued)*

Date	Smollett, Withdrawals Explanation	Post. Ref.	Debit	Credit	Acct. No. 320 Balance
1990					
Sept.					

Date	Cargo Fees Earned Explanation	Post. Ref.	Debit	Credit	Acct. No. 410 Balance
1990					
Sept.					

Date	Passenger Fees Earned Explanation	Post. Ref.	Debit	Credit	Acct. No. 420 Balance
1990					
Sept.					

Date	Salary Expense Explanation	Post. Ref.	Debit	Credit	Acct. No. 510 Balance
1990					
Sept.					

Date	Advertising Expense Explanation	Post. Ref.	Debit	Credit	Acct. No. 520 Balance
1990					
Sept.					

Date	Repairs Expense Explanation	Post. Ref.	Debit	Credit	Acct. No. 530 Balance
1990					
Sept.					

PROBLEM **A3-5**

Smollett Ships *(continued)*

Date		Miscellaneous Expense Explanation	Post. Ref.	Debit	Credit	Acct. No. 540 Balance
1990						
Sept.						

4.

SMOLLETT SHIPS Trial Balance September 30, 1990		

5.

SMOLLETT SHIPS Income Statement Month Ended September 30, 1990		

PROBLEM **A3-5**

Smollett Ships *(concluded)*

NAME

SECTION

DATE

SMOLLETT SHIPS **Statement of Owner's Equity** **Month Ended September 30, 1990**	

SMOLLETT SHIPS **Balance Sheet** **September 30, 1990**			
Assets		**Liabilities & Owner's Equity**	

PROBLEM **A3-6**

NAME
SECTION
DATE

Allardyce Repair Service

ALLARDYCE REPAIR SERVICE Trial Balance January 31, 1990		
Cash		
Accounts Receivable		
Office Supplies on Hand		
Prepaid Insurance		
Office Equipment		
Notes Payable		
Accounts Payable		
Allardyce, Capital		
Allardyce, Withdrawals		
Repair Revenue Earned		
Salary Expense		
Advertising Expense		
Totals		

PROBLEM **A4-2**

NAME
SECTION
DATE

Maclaren Company

1. **General Journal**

Date	Account Titles and Explanation	Post. Ref.	Debit	Credit
1990				
a.				
Feb.				
b.				
c.				
d.				
e.				
f.				
2.				
1990				
Mar.				

PROBLEM **A4-4**

Balfour Company

NAME

SECTION

DATE

1.

General Journal

Date	Account Titles and Explanation	Post. Ref.	Debit	Credit
1990				
a.				
June				
b.				
c.				
d.				
e.				

General Ledger

2.

Date	Cash	Post. Ref.	Debit	Credit	Acct. No. Balance

Date	Accounts Receivable	Post. Ref.	Debit	Credit	Acct. No. Balance

Date	Office Supplies on Hand	Post. Ref.	Debit	Credit	Acct. No. Balance

PROBLEM **A4-4**

Balfour Company *(continued)*

Date	Land	Post. Ref.	Debit	Credit	Acct. No. Balance

Date	Office Building	Post. Ref.	Debit	Credit	Acct. No. Balance

Date	Accum. Depr. Office Building	Post. Ref.	Debit	Credit	Acct. No. Balance

Date	Office Equipment	Post. Ref.	Debit	Credit	Acct. No. Balance

Date	Accum. Depr. Office Equip.	Post. Ref.	Debit	Credit	Acct. No. Balance

Date	Accounts Payable	Post. Ref.	Debit	Credit	Acct. No. Balance

PROBLEM **A4-4**

Balfour Company *(continued)*

NAME
SECTION
DATE

Date		Interest Payable	Post. Ref.	Debit	Credit	Acct. No. Balance

Date		Salaries Payable	Post. Ref.	Debit	Credit	Acct. No. Balance

Date		Unearned Revenue	Post. Ref.	Debit	Credit	Acct. No. Balance

Date		Notes Payable	Post. Ref.	Debit	Credit	Acct. No. Balance

Date		Balfour, Capital	Post. Ref.	Debit	Credit	Acct. No. Balance

Date		Balfour, Withdrawals	Post. Ref.	Debit	Credit	Acct. No. Balance

PROBLEM **A4-4**

Balfour Company *(continued)*

Date		Revenue	Post. Ref.	Debit	Credit	Acct. No. Balance

Date		Salary Expense	Post. Ref.	Debit	Credit	Acct. No. Balance

Date		Office Supplies Expense	Post. Ref.	Debit	Credit	Acct. No. Balance

Date		Deprec. Expense: Office Bldg.	Post. Ref.	Debit	Credit	Acct. No. Balance

PROBLEM **A4-4**

NAME
SECTION
DATE

Balfour Company *(continued)*

Date	Deprec. Expense: Office Equip.	Post. Ref.	Debit	Credit	Acct. No. Balance

Date	Interest Expense	Post. Ref.	Debit	Credit	Acct. No. Balance

Date	Utilities Expense	Post. Ref.	Debit	Credit	Acct. No. Balance

Date	Miscellaneous Expense	Post. Ref.	Debit	Credit	Acct. No. Balance

PROBLEM **A4-4**

Balfour Company *(continued)*

3. **BALFOUR COMPANY** **Adjusted Trial Balance** **June 30, 1990**		
Cash		
Accounts Receivable		
Office Supplies on Hand		
Land		
Office Building		
Accumulated Depreciation: Office Building		
Office Equipment		
Accumulated Depreciation.: Office Equipment		
Accounts Payable		
Interest Payable		
Salaries Payable		
Unearned Revenue		
Note Payable		
Balfour, Capita		
Balfour, Withdrawals		
Revenue		
Salary Expense		
Office Supplies Expense		
Depreciation Expense: Office Building		
Depreciation Expense: Office Equipment		
Interest Expense		
Utilities Expense		
Miscellaneous Expense		
Totals		

4. **BALFOUR COMPANY** **Income Statement** **Year Ended June 30, 1990**		
Revenue:		
Revenue		
Expenses:		
Salary Expense		
Office Supplies Expense		
Depreciation Expense: Office Building		
Depreciation Expense: Office Equipment		
Interest Expense		
Utilities Expense		
Miscellaneous Expense		
Total Expenses		
Net Income		

PROBLEM **A4-4**

Balfour Company *(concluded)*

NAME

SECTION

DATE

BALFOUR COMPANY Statement of Owner's Equity Year Ended June 30, 1990		
Balfour, Capital, July 1, 1989		
Add: Net Income		
Total		
Less: Withdrawals		
Balfour, Capital, June 30, 1990		

BALFOUR COMPANY Balance Sheet June 30, 1990			
Assets		**Liabilities & Owner's Equity**	
Current Assets:		Liabilities:	
Cash		Current Liabilities:	
Accounts Receivable		Accounts Payable	
Office Supplies on Hand		Interest Payable	
Total Current Assets		Salaries Payable	
		Unearned Revenue	
Property, Plant, and Equipment:		Total Current Liabilities	
Land			
Office Bldg.		Long-Term Liabilities:	
Less: Acc. Depr.		Notes Payable	
Office Equip.		Total Liabilities	
Less: Acc. Depr.			
Total Property,		Owner's Equity:	
Plant, and Equipment		Balfour, Capital	
		Total Liabilities and Owner's	
Total Assets		Equity	

PROBLEM **A4-5**

Red Fox Plumbing Company

NAME
SECTION
DATE

General Journal

Date		Account Titles and Explanation	Post. Ref.	Debit	Credit
1990					
Dec.	31				
	31				
	31				
	31				
	31				
	31				

PROBLEM **A4-6**

Alexander Balfour Company

NAME

SECTION

DATE

ALEXANDER BALFOUR COMPANY
Balance Sheet
December 31, 1990

Assets		Liabilities & Owner's Equity	
Current Assets:		Liabilities:	
		Current Liabilities:	
		Long-Term Liabilities:	
Investments:			
Property, Plant, and Equipment:		Owner's Equity:	
Intangibles:			
		Total Liabilities	
Total Assets		and Owner's Equity	

PROBLEM **A5-1**

Worksheet for this problem is at the back of this book.

NAME
SECTION
DATE

Danvers Carew Company *(continued)*

	General Journal			
Date	Account Titles and Explanation	Post. Ref.	Debit	Credit
	Adjusting Entries			

PROBLEM **A5-1**

Danvers Carew Company *(concluded)*

General Journal

Date	Account Titles and Explanation	Post. Ref.	Debit	Credit

PROBLEM **A5-3**

Worksheet for this problem is at the back of this book.

NAME

SECTION

DATE

Richard Enfield Company *(continued)*

RICHARD ENFIELD COMPANY
Income Statement
Year Ended December 31, 1990

RICHARD ENFIELD COMPANY
Statement of Owner's Equity
Year Ended December 31, 1990

PROBLEM **A5-3**

Richard Enfield Company *(continued)*

RICHARD ENFIELD COMPANY
Balance Sheet
December 31, 1990

RICHARD ENFIELD COMPANY
General Journal

Page

Date	Account Titles and Explanation	Post. Ref.	Debit	Credit
	Adjusting Entries			

PROBLEM **A5-3**

Richard Enfield Company *(continued)*

NAME
SECTION
DATE

General Journal

Page

Date	Account Titles and Explanation	Post. Ref.	Debit	Credit
	Closing Entries			

PROBLEM **A5-3**

Richard Enfield Company *(continued)*

General Ledger

Date		Cash Explanation	Post. Ref.	Debit	Credit	Acct. No. Balance

Date		Accounts Receivable Explanation	Post. Ref.	Debit	Credit	Acct. No. Balance

Date		Prepaid Insurance Explanation	Post. Ref.	Debit	Credit	Acct. No. Balance

Date		Store Supplies on Hand Explanation	Post. Ref.	Debit	Credit	Acct. No. Balance

Date		Land Explanation	Post. Ref.	Debit	Credit	Acct. No. Balance

Date		Store Building Explanation	Post. Ref.	Debit	Credit	Acct. No. Balance

PROBLEM **A5-3**

NAME

SECTION

DATE

Richard Enfield Company *(continued)*

Date		Accum. Depr.: Store Building Explanation	Post. Ref.	Debit	Credit	Acct. No. Balance

Date		Store Equipment Explanation	Post. Ref.	Debit	Credit	Acct. No. Balance

Date		Accum. Depr.: Store Equipment Explanation	Post. Ref.	Debit	Credit	Acct. No. Balance

Date		Accounts Payable Explanation	Post. Ref.	Debit	Credit	Acct. No. Balance

Date		Salaries Payable Explanation	Post. Ref.	Debit	Credit	Acct. No. Balance

Date		Interest Payable Explanation	Post. Ref.	Debit	Credit	Acct. No. Balance

PROBLEM **A5-3**

Richard Enfield Company *(continued)*

Date		Notes Payable Explanation	Post. Ref.	Debit	Credit	Acct. No. Balance

Date		Enfield, Capital Explanation	Post. Ref.	Debit	Credit	Acct. No. Balance

Date		Enfield, Withdrawals Explanation	Post. Ref.	Debit	Credit	Acct. No. Balance

Date		Expense and Revenue Summary Explanation	Post. Ref.	Debit	Credit	Acct. No. Balance

Date		Service Revenues Earned Explanation	Post. Ref.	Debit	Credit	Acct. No. Balance

Date		Salary Expense Explanation	Post. Ref.	Debit	Credit	Acct. No. Balance

PROBLEM **A5-3**

NAME
SECTION
DATE

Richard Enfield Company *(continued)*

Date	Professional Training Expenses Explanation	Post. Ref.	Debit	Credit	Acct. No. Balance

Date	Storage Rental Expense Explanation	Post. Ref.	Debit	Credit	Acct. No. Balance

Date	Repairs Expense Explanation	Post. Ref.	Debit	Credit	Acct. No. Balance

Date	Utilities Expense Explanation	Post. Ref.	Debit	Credit	Acct. No. Balance

Date	Telephone Expense Explanation	Post. Ref.	Debit	Credit	Acct. No. Balance

Date	Insurance Expense Explanation	Post. Ref.	Debit	Credit	Acct. No. Balance

PROBLEM **A5-3**

Richard Enfield Company *(continued)*

	Store Supplies Expense	Post.			Acct. No.
Date	Explanation	Ref.	Debit	Credit	Balance

	Depr. Expense: Store Building	Post.			Acct. No.
Date	Explanation	Ref.	Debit	Credit	Balance

	Depr. Expense: Store Equipment	Post.			Acct. No.
Date	Explanation	Ref.	Debit	Credit	Balance

	Interest Expense	Post.			Acct. No.
Date	Explanation	Ref.	Debit	Credit	Balance

PROBLEM **A5-3**

NAME
SECTION
DATE

Richard Enfield Company *(concluded)*

RICHARD ENFIELD COMPANY Post-Closing Trial Balance Year Ended December 31, 1990		
	Debit	Credit

NAME
SECTION
DATE

PROBLEM **A5-4**

Dr. Jenkins, M.D.

	General Journal			Page 1
Date	**Account Titles and Explanation**	**Post. Ref.**	**Debit**	**Credit**

PROBLEM **A5-4**

Dr. Jenkins, M.D. *(continued)*

General Journal

Date	Account Titles and Explanation	Post. Ref.	Debit	Credit

Adjusting Entries

Date	Account Titles and Explanation	Post. Ref.	Debit	Credit

PROBLEM **A5-4**

NAME
SECTION
DATE

Dr. Jenkins, M.D. *(continued)*

General Journal

Date		Account Titles and Explanation	Post. Ref.	Debit	Credit
		Closing Entries			
		Reversing Entries			

PROBLEM **A5-4**

Dr. Jenkins, M.D. *(continued)*

General Ledger

Date		Cash	Post. Ref.	Debit	Credit	Acct. No. 110 Balance

Date		Accounts Receivable	Post. Ref.	Debit	Credit	Acct. No. 120 Balance

Date		Medical Supplies on Hand	Post. Ref.	Debit	Credit	Acct. No. 130 Balance

Date		Prepaid Insurance	Post. Ref.	Debit	Credit	Acct. No. 140 Balance

Date		Land	Post. Ref.	Debit	Credit	Acct. No. 150 Balance

PROBLEM **A5-4**

NAME
SECTION
DATE

Dr. Jenkins, M.D. *(continued)*

Date	Medical Building	Post. Ref.	Debit	Credit	Acct. No. 160 Balance

Date	Accumulated Depreciation: Medical Building	Post. Ref.	Debit	Credit	Acct. No. 165 Balance

Date	Medical Equipment	Post. Ref.	Debit	Credit	Acct. No. 170 Balance

Date	Accumulated Depreciation: Medical Equipment	Post. Ref.	Debit	Credit	Acct. No. 175 Balance

Date	10% Notes Payable	Post. Ref.	Debit	Credit	Acct. No. 210 Balance

Date	Interest Payable	Post. Ref.	Debit	Credit	Acct. No. 220 Balance

PROBLEM **A5-4**

Dr. Jenkins, M.D. *(continued)*

Date		Accounts Payable	Post. Ref.	Debit	Credit	Acct. No. 230 Balance

Date		Salaries Payable	Post. Ref.	Debit	Credit	Acct. No. 240 Balance

Date		Unearned Research Fees	Post. Ref.	Debit	Credit	Acct. No. 250 Balance

Date		12% Note Payable	Post. Ref.	Debit	Credit	Acct. No. 260 Balance

Date		Jenkins, Capital	Post. Ref.	Debit	Credit	Acct. No. 310 Balance

Date		Jenkins, Withdrawals	Post. Ref.	Debit	Credit	Acct. No. 320 Balance

PROBLEM **A5-4**

NAME
SECTION
DATE

Dr. Jenkins, M.D. *(continued)*

Date		Expense and Revenue Summary	Post. Ref.	Debit	Credit	Acct. No. 330 Balance

Date		Medical Fees Earned	Post. Ref.	Debit	Credit	Acct. No. 410 Balance

Date		Research Fees Earned	Post. Ref.	Debit	Credit	Acct. No. 420 Balance

Date		Salary Expense	Post. Ref.	Debit	Credit	Acct. No. 510 Balance

PROBLEM **A5-4**

Dr. Jenkins, M.D. *(continued)*

Date		Insurance Expense	Post. Ref.	Debit	Credit	Acct. No. 520 Balance

Date		Repairs Expense	Post. Ref.	Debit	Credit	Acct. No. 530 Balance

Date		Medical Supplies Expense	Post. Ref.	Debit	Credit	Acct. No. 540 Balance

Date		Medical Association Dues Expense	Post. Ref.	Debit	Credit	Acct. No. 550 Balance

PROBLEM **A5-4**

Dr. Jenkins, M.D. *(continued)*

NAME

SECTION

DATE

Date	Depreciation Expense: Medical Building	Post. Ref.	Debit	Credit	Acct. No. 560 Balance

Date	Depreciation Expense Medical Equipment	Post. Ref.	Debit	Credit	Acct. No. 570 Balance

Date	Interest Expense	Post. Ref.	Debit	Credit	Acct. No. 580 Balance

Date	Telephone Expense	Post. Ref.	Debit	Credit	Acct. No. 590 Balance

PROBLEM **A5-4**

Dr. Jenkins, M.D. *(continued)*

Worksheet for this problem is at the back of this book.

DR. JENKINS, M.D.
Income Statement
Month Ended October 31, 1990

DR. JENKINS, M.D.
Statement of Owner's Equity
Month Ended October 31, 1990

PROBLEM **A5-4**

Dr. Jenkins, M.D. *(concluded)*

Worksheet for problem A5-5 is at the back of this book.

NAME

SECTION

DATE

DR. JENKINS, M.D. Balance Sheet October 31, 1990			
Assets		**Liabilities & Owner's Equity**	

DR. JENKINS, M.D. Post-Closing Trial Balance October 31, 1990		

PROBLEM **A6-1**

NAME
SECTION
DATE

Billy Bigelow Carousel Company

BILLY BIGELOW CAROUSEL COMPANY
Income Statement
Year Ended June 30, 1990

PROBLEM **A6-2**

NAME
SECTION
DATE

The Hammerstein Company

1.	THE HAMMERSTEIN COMPANY			
	General Journal	Post.		
Date	Account Titles and Explanation	Ref.	Debit	Credit

PROBLEM **A6-2**

The Hammerstein Company *(concluded)*

2.

THE ROGERS COMPANY

General Journal

Date		Account Titles and Explanation	Post. Ref.	Debit	Credit
1990					
June					

PROBLEM **A6-3**

Worksheet for this problem is at the back of this book.

NAME
SECTION
DATE

The Molnar Company *(concluded)*

Date		General Journal Account Titles and Explanation	Post. Ref.	Debit	Credit
		Closing Entries			
1990					
Dec.					

PROBLEM **A6-4**

Worksheet for this problem is at the back of this book.

NAME
SECTION
DATE

The New England Sales Company *(continued)*

2.

NEW ENGLAND SALES COMPANY
Income Statement
Year Ended December 31, 1990

NEW ENGLAND SALES COMPANY
Statement of Changes in Owner's Equity
Year Ended December 31, 1990

PROBLEM **A6-4**

The New England Sales Company *(continued)*

NEW ENGLAND SALES COMPANY Balance Sheet December 31, 1990			
Assets		**Liabilities & Owner's Equity**	

PROBLEM **A6-4**

NAME
SECTION
DATE

The New England Sales Company *(continued)*

3. **General Journal**

Date	Account Titles and Explanation	Post. Ref.	Debit	Credit
	Adjusting Entries			
	Closing Entries			

PROBLEM **A6-4**

The New England Sales Company *(concluded)*

General Journal

Date	Account Titles and Explanation	Post. Ref.	Debit	Credit
1990				
Dec.				

PROBLEM **A7-1**

Grangerford Company

NAME
SECTION
DATE

PROBLEM **A7-2**

Southern Nittany Tigers

NAME
SECTION
DATE

PROBLEM **A7-3**

Sherburn Company

NAME

SECTION

DATE

1.

Sales Journal

Date	Account Debited	Invoice Number	Post. Ref.	Amount
1990				
Oct.				

Purchases Journal

Date	Account Credited	Invoice Date	Post. Ref.	Amount
1990				
Oct.				

General Journal

Date	Account Titles and Explanation	Post. Ref.	Debit	Credit
1990				
Oct.				

PROBLEM **A7-3**

Sherburn Company *(continued)*

General Ledger

2.		Accounts Receivable	Post.			Acct. No. 120
Date		Explanation	Ref.	Debit	Credit	Balance
1990						
Oct.						

		Accounts Payable	Post.			Acct. No. 210
Date		Explanation	Ref.	Debit	Credit	Balance
1990						
Oct.						

		Sales	Post.			Acct. No. 410
Date		Explanation	Ref.	Debit	Credit	Balance
1990						
Oct.						

		Sales Returns and Allowances	Post.			Acct. No. 420
Date		Explanation	Ref.	Debit	Credit	Balance
1990						
Oct.						

		Purchases	Post.			Acct. No. 510
Date		Explanation	Ref.	Debit	Credit	Balance
1990						
Oct.						

		Purchases Returns and Allow.	Post.			Acct. No. 520
Date		Explanation	Ref.	Debit	Credit	Balance
1990						
Oct.						

PROBLEM **A7-3**

Sherburn Company *(continued)*

NAME

SECTION

DATE

Accounts Receivable Ledger

Date	Loftus Company Explanation	Post. Ref.	Debit	Credit	Balance
1990					
Oct.					

Date	Thatcher Company Explanation	Post. Ref.	Debit	Credit	Balance
1990					
Oct.					

Date	Turner Company Explanation	Post. Ref.	Debit	Credit	Balance
1990					
Oct.					

Date	Wilks, Ltd. Explanation	Post. Ref.	Debit	Credit	Balance
1990					
Oct.					

PROBLEM **A7-3**

Sherburn Company *(continued)*

Accounts Payable Ledger

Date		Barnes and Associates Explanation	Post. Ref.	Debit	Credit	Balance
1990 Oct.						

Date		Harkness Company Explanation	Post. Ref.	Debit	Credit	Balance
1990 Oct.						

Date		Phelps, Inc. Explanation	Post. Ref.	Debit	Credit	Balance
1990 Oct.						

Date		Watson and Son Explanation	Post. Ref.	Debit	Credit	Balance
1990 Oct.						

PROBLEM **A7-3**

NAME
SECTION
DATE

Sherburn Company *(concluded)*

3.

SHERBURN COMPANY Schedule of Accounts Receivable October 31, 1990	
Loftus Company	
Thatcher Company	
Turner Company	
Wilks, Ltd.	
Total	

SHERBURN COMPANY Schedule of Accounts Payable October 31, 1990	
Barnes and Associates	
Harkness Company	
Phelps, Inc.	
Watson and Son	
Total	

PROBLEM **A7-4**

Levi Bell Company

NAME

SECTION

DATE

Cash Receipts Journal

Date	Account Credited	Post. Ref.	Sundry Accounts Cr.	Accounts Receivable Cr	Sales Cr.	Sales Discounts Dr.	Cash Dr.	
1990								
Nov.								

PROBLEM **A7-4**

Levi Bell Company *(concluded)*

Cash Payments Journal

Date	Check Number	Account Debited	Post. Ref.	Sundry Accounts Debit	Accounts Payable Debit	Purchases Debit	Purchases Discounts Credit	Cash Credit
1990								
Nov.								

PROBLEM **A7-5**

Riverson Company

NAME
SECTION
DATE

Date		Sales Journal Account Debited	Invoice Number	Post. Ref.	Page 32 Amount
1990					
Dec.					

Date		General Journal Account Titles and Explanation	Post. Ref.	Debit	Page 18 Credit
1990					
Dec.					

PROBLEM **A7-5**

Riverson Company *(continued)*

Cash Receipts Journal

Date	Account Credited	Post. Ref.	Sundry Accounts Credit	Accounts Receivable Credit	Sales Credit	Sales Discount Debit	Cash Debit	
1990								
Dec.								

PROBLEM **A7-5**

NAME

SECTION

DATE

Riverson Company *(continued)*

General Ledger

Date	Cash Explanation	Post. Ref.	Debit	Credit	Acct. No. 110 Balance
1990					
Dec.					

Date	Accounts Receivable Explanation	Post. Ref.	Debit	Credit	Acct. No. 120 Balance
1990					
Dec.					

Date	Notes Payable Explanation	Post. Ref.	Debit	Credit	Acct. No. 210 Balance
1990					
Dec.					

Date	Riverson, Capital Explanation	Post. Ref.	Debit	Credit	Acct. No. 310 Balance
1990					
Dec.					

PROBLEM **A7-5**

Riverson Company *(continued)*

Date		Sales Explanation	Post. Ref.	Debit	Credit	Acct. No. 410 Balance
1990						
Dec.						

Date		Sales Returns and Allowances Explanation	Post. Ref.	Debit	Credit	Acct. No. 420 Balance
1990						
Dec.						

Date		Sales Discounts Explanation	Post. Ref.	Debit	Credit	Acct. No. 430 Balance
1990						
Dec.						

Date		Explanation	Post. Ref.	Debit	Credit	Acct. No. Balance

PROBLEM **A7-5**

Riverson Company *(concluded)*

NAME

SECTION

DATE

Accounts Receivable Ledger

Date		Baker, J. Explanation	Post. Ref.	Debit	Credit	Balance
1990						
Dec.						

Date		Harper, S. Explanation	Post. Ref.	Debit	Credit	Balance
1990						
Dec.						

Date		Miller, G. Explanation	Post. Ref.	Debit	Credit	Balance
1990						
Dec.						

Date		Rogers, S. Explanation	Post. Ref.	Debit	Credit	Balance
1990						
Dec.						

RIVERSON COMPANY Schedule of Accounts Receivable December 31, 1990	
Baker, J.	
Miller, G.	
Rogers, S.	
Total	

PROBLEM **A7-6**

NAME
SECTION
DATE

Robinson Company

Date		Purchases Journal Account Credited	Invoice Date	Post. Ref.	Page 17 Amount
1990					
Jan.					

Date		General Journal Account Titles and Explanation	Post. Ref.	Debit	Page 11 Credit
1990					
Jan.					

PROBLEM **A7-6**

Robinson Company *(continued)*

Cash Payments Journal

Date	Check Number	Account Debited	Post. Ref.	Sundry Accounts Debit	Accounts Payable Debit	Purchases Debit	Purchase Discounts Credit	Cash Credit
1990								
Jan.								

PROBLEM **A7-6**

NAME
SECTION
DATE

Robinson Company *(continued)*

General Ledger

Date	Cash Explanation	Post. Ref.	Debit	Credit	Acct. No. 110 Balance
1990					
Jan.					

Date	Accounts Payable Explanation	Post. Ref.	Debit	Credit	Acct. No. 210 Balance
1990					
Jan.					

Date	Robinson, Withdrawals Explanation	Post. Ref.	Debit	Credit	Acct. No. 320 Balance
1990					
Jan.					

Date	Purchases Explanation	Post. Ref.	Debit	Credit	Acct. No. 510 Balance
1990					
Jan.					

PROBLEM **A7-6**

Robinson Company *(continued)*

Date		Purchases Returns and Allow. Explanation	Post. Ref.	Debit	Credit	Acct. No. 520 Balance
1990						
Jan.						

Date		Purchases Discounts Explanation	Post. Ref.	Debit	Credit	Acct. No. 530 Balance
1990						
Jan.						

Date		Freight-In Explanation	Post. Ref.	Debit	Credit	Acct. No. 540 Balance
1990						
Jan.						

Date		Salary Expense Explanation	Post. Ref.	Debit	Credit	Acct. No. 610 Balance
1990						
Jan.						

PROBLEM **A7-6**

NAME
SECTION
DATE

Robinson Company *(concluded)*

Accounts Payable Ledger

Date	Finn Company Explanation	Post. Ref.	Debit	Credit	Balance
1990					
Jan.					

Date	Sawyer, Inc. Explanation	Post. Ref.	Debit	Credit	Balance
1990					
Jan.					

Date	Thatcher Company Explanation	Post. Ref.	Debit	Credit	Balance
1990					
Jan.					

Date	Twain Company Explanation	Post. Ref.	Debit	Credit	Balance
1990					
Jan.					

ROBINSON COMPANY Schedule of Accounts Payable January 31, 1990	
Finn Company	
Thatcher Company	
Twain Company	
Total	

PROBLEM **A7-7**

Dobbins Company

NAME

SECTION

DATE

2.		Sales Journal			Page 15
			Invoice	Post.	
Date		Account Debited	Number	Ref.	Amount
1990					
Jan.					

		Purchases Journal			Page 22
			Invoice	Post.	
Date		Account Credited	Date	Ref.	Amount
1990					
Jan.					

PROBLEM **A7-7**

Dobbins Company *(continued)*

Cash Receipts Journal

Page 31

Date	Account Credited	Post. Ref.	Sundry Accounts Credit	Accounts Receivable Credit	Sales Credit	Sales Discounts Debit	Cash Debit	
1990								
Jan.								

Cash Payments Journal

Page 42

Date	Check Number	Account Debited	Post. Ref.	Sundry Accounts Debit	Accounts Payable Debit	Purchases Debit	Purchase Discounts Credit	Cash Credit
1990								
Jan.								

PROBLEM **A7-7**

Dobbins Company *(continued)*

NAME
SECTION
DATE

Date	General Journal Account Titles and Explanation	Post. Ref.	Debit	Credit
				Page 13
1990				
Jan.				

8.

Date	General Journal Account Titles and Explanation	Post. Ref.	Debit	Credit
	Adjusting Entries			
1990				
Jan.				

PROBLEM **A7-7**

Dobbins Company *(continued)*

General Journal				
Date	Account Titles and Explanation	Post. Ref.	Debit	Credit
	Closing Entries			
1990				
Jan.				

PROBLEM **A7-7**

Worksheet for this problem is at the back of this book.

NAME
SECTION
DATE

Dobbins Company *(continued)*

General Ledger

1. and 3.

Cash Date		Explanation	Post. Ref.	Debit	Credit	Acct. No. 110 Balance
1990						
Jan.						

Accounts Receivable Date		Explanation	Post. Ref.	Debit	Credit	Acct. No. 120 Balance
1990						
Jan.						

Merchandise Inventory Date		Explanation	Post. Ref.	Debit	Credit	Acct. No. 130 Balance
1990						
Jan.						

Prepaid Rent on Hand Date		Explanation	Post. Ref.	Debit	Credit	Acct. No. 140 Balance
1990						
Jan.						

Office Supplies on Hand Date		Explanation	Post. Ref.	Debit	Credit	Acct. No. 150 Balance
1990						
Jan.						

Office Equipment Date		Explanation	Post. Ref.	Debit	Credit	Acct. No. 160 Balance
1990						
Jan.						

PROBLEM **A7-7**

Dobbins Company *(continued)*

Date		Accumulated Depreciation Explanation	Post. Ref.	Debit	Credit	Acct. No. 165 Balance
1990						
Jan.						

Date		Notes Payable Explanation	Post. Ref.	Debit	Credit	Acct. No. 210 Balance
1990						
Jan.						

Date		Accounts Payable Explanation	Post. Ref.	Debit	Credit	Acct. No. 220 Balance
1990						
Jan.						

Date		Salaries Payable Explanation	Post. Ref.	Debit	Credit	Acct. No. 230 Balance
1990						
Jan.						

Date		Dobbins, Capital Explanation	Post. Ref.	Debit	Credit	Acct. No. 310 Balance
1990						
Jan.						

Date		Dobbins, Withdrawals Explanation	Post. Ref.	Debit	Credit	Acct. No. 320 Balance
1990						
Jan.						

PROBLEM **A7-7**

NAME

SECTION

DATE

Dobbins Company *(continued)*

Date		Expense and Revenue Summary Explanation	Post. Ref.	Debit	Credit	Acct. No. 330 Balance
1990						
Jan.						

Date		Sales Explanation	Post. Ref.	Debit	Credit	Acct. No. 410 Balance
1990						
Jan.						

Date		Sales Returns and Allowances Explanation	Post. Ref.	Debit	Credit	Acct. No. 420 Balance
1990						
Jan.						

Date		Sales Discounts Explanation	Post. Ref.	Debit	Credit	Acct. No. 430 Balance
1990						
Jan.						

Date		Purchases Explanation	Post. Ref.	Debit	Credit	Acct. No. 510 Balance
1990						
Jan.						

Date		Purchases Returns and Allow. Explanation	Post. Ref.	Debit	Credit	Acct. No. 520 Balance
1990						
Jan.						

PROBLEM **A7-7**

Dobbins Company *(continued)*

Date		Purchases Discounts Explanation	Post. Ref.	Debit	Credit	Acct. No. 530 Balance
1990						
Jan.						

Date		Freight-In Explanation	Post. Ref.	Debit	Credit	Acct. No. 540 Balance
1990						
Jan.						

Date		Salary Expense Explanation	Post. Ref.	Debit	Credit	Acct. No. 610 Balance
1990						
Jan.						

Date		Rent Expense Explanation	Post. Ref.	Debit	Credit	Acct. No. 620 Balance
1990						
Jan.						

Date		Office Supplies Expense Explanation	Post. Ref.	Debit	Credit	Acct. No. 630 Balance
1990						
Jan.						

Date		Depreciation Expense Explanation	Post. Ref.	Debit	Credit	Acct. No. 640 Balance
1990						
Jan.						

PROBLEM **A7-7**

NAME
SECTION
DATE

Dobbins Company *(continued)*

Date		Interest Exp.: Explanation	Post. Ref.	Debit	Credit	Acct. No. 650 Balance
1990						
Jan.						

Accounts Receivable Subsidiary Ledger

Date		Douglas, W. Explanation	Post. Ref.	Debit	Credit	Balance
1990						
Jan.						

Date		Polly, A. Explanation	Post. Ref.	Debit	Credit	Balance
1990						
Jan.						

Date		Potter, M. Explanation	Post. Ref.	Debit	Credit	Balance
1990						
Jan.						

Date		Sprauge, R. Explanation	Post. Ref.	Debit	Credit	Balance
1990						
Jan.						

PROBLEM **A7-7**

Dobbins Company *(continued)*

Accounts Payable Subsidiary Ledger

Date		Boggs, Inc. Explanation	Post. Ref.	Debit	Credit	Balance
1990						
Jan.						

Date		Frazer Company Explanation	Post. Ref.	Debit	Credit	Balance
1990						
Jan.						

Date		Phelps, Inc. Explanation	Post. Ref.	Debit	Credit	Balance
1990						
Jan.						

Date		Watson Company Explanation	Post. Ref.	Debit	Credit	Balance
1990						
Jan.						

PROBLEM **A7-7**

Dobbins Company *(continued)*

NAME

SECTION

DATE

7.

DOBBINS COMPANY
Income Statement
Month Ended January 31, 1990

DOBBINS COMPANY
Statement of Owner's Equity
Month Ended January 31, 1990

PROBLEM **A7-7**

Dobbins Company *(concluded)*

DOBBINS COMPANY
Balance Sheet
January 31, 1990

Assets		Liabilities & Owner's Equity	

9.

DOBBINS COMPANY
Schedule of Accounts Receivable
January 31, 1990

Polly, A.	
Potter, M.	
Sprauge, R.	
Total	

DOBBINS COMPANY
Schedule of Accounts Payable
January 31, 1990

Boggs, Inc.	
Frazer Company	
Phelps, Inc.	
Watson Company	
Total	

PROBLEM **A8-2**

Jay Watson Company

NAME

SECTION

DATE

1. JAY WATSON COMPANY Bank Reconciliation February 28, 1990		

Date	General Journal Account Titles and Explanation	Post. Ref.	Debit	Credit
1990				

PROBLEM **A8-3**

Delta Co.

NAME
SECTION
DATE

Date	General Journal Account Titles and Explanation	Post. Ref.	Debit	Credit
1991				

PROBLEM **A8-3**

Delta Co. *(concluded)*

Date		General Journal Account Titles and Explanation	Post. Ref.	Debit	Credit
1991					

PROBLEM **A8-4**

NAME
SECTION
DATE

Vickers Shoes

1. Gross method	**General Journal**			
		Post.		
Date	**Account Titles and Explanation**	**Ref.**	**Debit**	**Credit**
1991				

PROBLEM **A8-4**

Vickers Shoes *(continued)*

2. VICKERS SHOES Income Statement For Month Ended January 31, 1991		

3. Net method	General Journal			
Date	Account Titles and Explanation	Post. Ref.	Debit	Credit
1991				

PROBLEM **A8-4**

Vickers Shoes *(continued)*

NAME

SECTION

DATE

Date		General Journal Account Titles and Explanation	Post. Ref.	Debit	Credit
1991					

PROBLEM **A8-4**

Vickers Shoes *(concluded)*

4.

VICKERS SHOES
Income Statement
For Month Ended January 31, 1991

PROBLEM **A8-5**

Voucher register for this problem is at the back of this book.

NAME
SECTION
DATE

Ruskin Supply Company *(concluded)*

RUSKIN SUPPLY COMPANY
Check Register

Date	Check Number	Payee	Vou. No.	Vouchers Payable Debit	Purchases Discounts Credit	Cash Credit
1991						

General Journal

Date	Account Titles and Explanation	Post. Ref.	Debit	Credit
1991				

PROBLEM **A9-1**

McGee Security Company

NAME
SECTION
DATE

1.

Date		General Journal Account Titles and Explanation	Post. Ref.	Debit	Credit
1989					

PROBLEM **A9-1**

McGee Security Company *(continued)*

	General Journal			
		Post.		
Date	Account Titles and Explanation	Ref.	Debit	Credit

PROBLEM **A9-1**

NAME
SECTION
DATE

McGee Security Company *(concluded)*

2. **Accounts Receivable**

Allowance for Uncollectible Accounts

PROBLEM **A9-2**

Browning Barricades Company

NAME
SECTION
DATE

PROBLEM **A9-4**

Maple Creek Office Supply Co.

NAME
SECTION
DATE

Date		General Journal Account Titles and Explanation	Post. Ref.	Debit	Credit
1990					

NAME
SECTION
DATE

PROBLEM **A9-5**

Boswell Refrigeration

1.

2.

Date		General Journal Account Titles and Explanation	Post. Ref.	Debit	Credit
1990					

PROBLEM **A9-6**

NAME
SECTION
DATE

Montana Equipment Company

1.

Date		General Journal Account Titles and Explanation	Post. Ref.	Debit	Credit
1990					

PROBLEM **A9-6**

Montana Equipment Company *(concluded)*

Date	Account Titles and Explanation	Post. Ref.	Debit	Credit
1990				
2.				

PROBLEM **A9-7**

NAME
SECTION
DATE

Custer's Sporting Goods

1.	General Journal			
		Post.		
Date	Account Titles and Explanation	Ref.	Debit	Credit
1990				

PROBLEM **A9-7**

Custer's Sporting Goods *(concluded)*

Date		Account Titles and Explanation	Post. Ref.	Debit	Credit
1990					
2.					

3.

CUSTER'S SPORTING GOODS
Partial Balance Sheet
January 31, 1990

Calculations:		

PROBLEM **A9-8**

NAME
SECTION
DATE

Columbia Equipment Co.

1. Name of Company's Stock Owned	Original Cost	Market Value Dec. 31, 1990

Calculation of cost and market value of each stock owned:

2. Date	General Journal Account Titles and Explanation	Post. Ref.	Debit	Credit
1990				
3.				

PROBLEM **A10-2**

Northport Electronics

NAME
SECTION
DATE

1.

NORTHPORT ELECTRONICS
Calculation of Ending Inventory and Cost of Goods Sold
Using FIFO, LIFO, and Weighted Average

	Units	Cost per Unit	Total Cost
	Gross Units Sold	**Less Returns**	**Net Units Sold**

PROBLEM **A10-2**

Northport Electronics *(concluded)*

PROBLEM **A10-3**

Brandon Paint Store

NAME
SECTION
DATE

Description	(A) Inventory Stock No.	(B) Quantity	(C) Cost Cost (FIFO)	(D) Market	(E) Item-by-Item LCM	
Paint						
Brushes						
Ladders						
Totals						
1. LCM ending inventory item-by-item basis (total of column E)						
2. LCM for inventory as a whole (smaller of column C and column D totals)						

PROBLEM **A10-4**

Mark's Hobby Store

NAME

SECTION

DATE

PROBLEM **A10-5**

Macho Sportswear

NAME

SECTION

DATE

MACHO SPORTSWEAR Calculation of Ending Inventory Using Retail Inventory Method January 31, 1991	Cost	Retail

PROBLEM **A10-6**

Paul's Pets

NAME

SECTION

DATE

1.

Calculation of Ending Inventory
Using Retail Inventory Method
April 30, 1990

	Cost	Retail

2.

PAUL'S PETS
Income Statement
Period July 1, 1989–April 30, 1990

PROBLEM **A10-6**

Paul's Pets *(concluded)*

3.

PAUL'S PETS
Balance Sheet
April 30, 1990

Assets

Liabilities & Owner's Equity

PROBLEM **A10-7**

NAME
SECTION
DATE

Otter Inc.

Calculation of Corrected Net Income for Each of 4 Years

Description	1988	1989	1990	1991
Net income reported	$34500	$ 19200	$(4000)	$ 15000
a. 1988 ending inventory overstated; 1989 beginning inventory overstated	(4200)	4200		

PROBLEM **A10-9**

Cascade Co.

Foldout working papers for problem A10-8 are at the back of this book.

NAME
SECTION
DATE

FIFO Perpetual Inventory:

Item: Canoe Paddle #CX789

Date	PURCHASES			COST OF GOODS SOLD			INVENTORY ON HAND		
	Quantity	Unit Cost	Total Cost	Quantity	Unit Cost	Total Cost	Quantity	Unit Cost	Total Cost

PROBLEM **A10-9**

Cascade Co. *(continued)*

LIFO Perpetual Inventory:

Item: Canoe Paddle #CX789

Date	PURCHASES			COST OF GOODS SOLD			INVENTORY ON HAND		
	Quantity	Unit Cost	Total Cost	Quantity	Unit Cost	Total Cost	Quantity	Unit Cost	Total Cost

PROBLEM **A10-9**

Cascade Co. *(concluded)*

NAME

SECTION

DATE

FIFO ending inventory:

FIFO cost of goods sold:

LIFO ending inventory:

LIFO cost of goods sold:

PROBLEM **A11-1**

Corts Corp.

NAME
SECTION
DATE

Description	Land	Buildings	Machinery	Land Improvements	Other Accounts Name	Other Accounts Amount

PROBLEM **A11-1**

Corts Corp. *(concluded)*

PROBLEM **A11-3**

Conraid Corp.

NAME

SECTION

DATE

Shredder — straight-line depreciation:

Copying machine — sum-of-the-years'-digits depreciation:

PROBLEM **A11-4**

Core Engineering

NAME
SECTION
DATE

General Journal

Date	Account Titles and Explanation	Post. Ref.	Debit	Credit
1989				

PROBLEM **A11-4**

Core Engineering *(concluded)*

PROPERTY, PLANT, AND EQUIPMENT SUBSIDIARY LEDGER RECORD

Asset: ____________________ **General Ledger Account:** ____________________

Identification No.: ____________________ **Mfg. Serial No.:** ____________________

Location: ____________________

Acquired from: ____________________ **Brand:** ____________________

Responsible Person: ____________________

Est. Life: ____________ **Salvage Value:** ____________ **Depr. Method:** ____________

Depr. Per Year: ____________ **Depr. Per Month:** ____________

Date	P/R	Asset			Accumulated Depreciation			Book Value
		Debit	Credit	Balance	Debit	Credit	Balance	

PROBLEM **A11-5**

Kiwi Restaurant Corp.

NAME

SECTION

DATE

General Journal

Date	Account Titles and Explanation	Post. Ref.	Debit	Credit
a.				
1991				
b.				
c.				

PROBLEM **A11-5**

Kiwi Restaurant Corp. *(concluded)*

	General Journal			
Date	**Account Titles and Explanation**	**Post. Ref.**	**Debit**	**Credit**
1991				

PROBLEM **A11-6**

DeAngelo's Garage

NAME

SECTION

DATE

	General Journal			
Date	Account Titles and Explanation	Post. Ref.	Debit	Credit
1990				

PROBLEM **A11-6**

DeAngelo's Garage *(concluded)*

General Journal				
Date	**Account Titles and Explanation**	**Post. Ref.**	**Debit**	**Credit**
1990				

PROBLEM **A11-7**

Barney's Mobile Lunch

NAME
SECTION
DATE

General Journal

Date	Account Titles and Explanation	Post. Ref.	Debit	Credit
1990				

PROBLEM **A11-7**

Barney's Mobile Lunch *(concluded)*

Date	General Journal Account Titles and Explanation	Post. Ref.	Debit	Credit
1991				

PROBLEM **A11-8**

Pioneer Corp.

NAME
SECTION
DATE

1.	**General Journal**			
Date	**Account Titles and Explanation**	**Post. Ref.**	**Debit**	**Credit**
1990				

PROBLEM **A12-2**

Maryland Corporation

NAME
SECTION
DATE

Date		General Journal Account Titles and Explanation	Post. Ref.	Debit	Credit
1990					
Sept.					

PROBLEM **A12-3**

Voucher register for this problem is at the back of this book.

NAME
SECTION
DATE

Hall Advertising Agency *(concluded)*

HALL ADVERTISING AGENCY
Check Register

Date	Check Number	Payee	Vouch. No.	Vouchers Payable Debit	Purchases Discount Credit	Cash Credit
Oct.						

General Journal

Date	Account Titles and Explanation	Post. Ref.	Debit	Credit
1990				
Oct.				

PROBLEM **A12-4**

The Atlanta Production Company

NAME
SECTION
DATE

1.

THE ATLANTA PRODUCTION COMPANY
Payroll Register
For the Week Ended November 9, 1990

Employee	Total Hours	Earnings			Taxable Earnings	
		Regular	Overtime	Total	FICA	Unemployment Compensation
Clayton, Adam						
Cobb, Betty						
DeKalb, Charles						
Fulton, Diane						
Gwinnett, Edward						
Henry, Fawn						

Deductions						Payment		Distribution	
FIT	FICA	Union Dues	Health Insurance	U.S. Savings Bonds	Total	Net Pay	Check No.	Office Salaries	Production Salaries

PROBLEM **A12-4**

The Atlanta Production Company *(concluded)*

2.	General Journal			
Date	Account Titles and Explanation	Post. Ref.	Debit	Credit
1990				
Nov.				

PROBLEM **A12-5**

Charles Litman

NAME
SECTION
DATE

1. and **2.**

NAME	Litman, Charles	TELEPHONE	(212) 512-3045	SOCIAL SECURITY NUMBER	196-16-3142
ADDRESS	1220 Avenue of the Americas New York, New York 10020	DATE EMPLOYED	May 12, 1979	DATE OF BIRTH	October 22, 1949
DATE TERMINATED		REASON			
MARRIED	(XX)				
SINGLE	( )	PAY RATE	$25,000		
HEAD OF HOUSEHOLD	( )	HOURLY PAY	$12.50		
DEPARTMENT	Shipping				

1990 Period Ending	Earnings					Deductions						Net Pay	Check No.
	Total Hours	Regular Hours	Overtime Hours	Total	Cumulative	FIT	FICA	Union Dues	Health Ins.	U.S. Bonds	Total		
Jan. 12	80	1,000.00		1,000.00	1,000.00	103.00	75.00	5.00	15.35		193.35	806.65	129
26	80	1,000.00		1,000.00	2,000.00	103.00	75.00	5.00	15.35		193.35	806.65	365
Feb. 9	80	1,000.00		1,000.00	3,000.00	103.00	75.00	5.00	15.35		193.35	806.65	494
23	92	1,000.00	225.00	1,225.00	4,225.00	136.00	91.88	5.00	15.35		248.23	976.77	609
Mar. 9	80	1,000.00		1,000.00	5,225.00	103.00	75.00	5.00	15.35		193.35	806.65	762
23													
1st Qtr.													

PROBLEM **A12-7**

NAME
SECTION
DATE

Atwell Appliance Company

Date		General Journal Account Titles and Explanation	Post. Ref.	Debit	Credit
1989					
Jan.	1				
to					
June	30				
July	1				
to					
Dec.	31				
Dec.	31				
1990					
Jan.	1				
to					
June	30				

PROBLEM **A13-2**

Moon, Engle, and Seibel

NAME

SECTION

DATE

Computation of Profit Distribution

	Moon	Engle	Seibel	Total
1.				
2.				
3.				
4.				

PROBLEM **A13-3**

NAME
SECTION
DATE

Reagan, Carter, and Ford

REAGAN, CARTER, AND FORD
Income Distribution Schedule
For the Year Ended December 31, 19XX

	Reagan	Carter	Ford	Total
1.				

	Reagan	Carter	Ford	Total
2.				

	Reagan	Carter	Ford	Total
3.				

PROBLEM **A13-4**

Piper and Peters

NAME
SECTION
DATE

Date		Account Titles and Explanation	Post. Ref.	Debit	Credit
1.					
2.					

PROBLEM **A13-5**

Poof Magic Store

NAME
SECTION
DATE

1.

POOF MAGIC STORE
Income Statement
Year Ended December 31, 1990

2.

POOF MAGIC STORE
Statement of Partners' Capital Accounts
Year Ended December 31, 1990

	Houdini	Merlin	Carson	Totals

PROBLEM **A13-5**

Poof Magic Store *(concluded)*

3.

POOF MAGIC STORE
Balance Sheet
December 31, 1990

Assets		Liabilities and Partners' Capital	

PROBLEM **A13-6**

NAME
SECTION
DATE

Steele, Yum, and Blind, CPAs

Date	General Journal Account Titles and Explanation	Post. Ref.	Debit	Credit
1.				
2.				
3.				
4.				

PROBLEM **A13-7**

Garcia, Johnson, and Steinberg

NAME
SECTION
DATE

General Journal				
Date	Account Titles and Explanation	Post. Ref.	Debit	Credit

PROBLEM **A13-7**

Garcia, Johnson, and Steinberg *(concluded)*

General Journal

Date		Account Titles and Explanation	Post. Ref.	Debit	Credit

PROBLEM **A13-8**

Mural, Lynched, and Smythe

NAME
SECTION
DATE

1\.

MURAL, LYNCHED, AND SMYTHE
Partnership Liquidation Schedule

	Cash	+	Other Assets	=	Accounts Payable	+	Mural, Capital	+	Lynched, Capital	+	Smythe, Capital

2\.

MURAL, LYNCHED, AND SMYTHE
Partnership Liquidation Schedule

	Cash	+	Other Assets	=	Accounts Payable	+	Mural, Capital	+	Lynched, Capital	+	Smythe, Capital

PROBLEM **A13-8**

Mural, Lynched, and Smythe *(concluded)*

3.

MURAL, LYNCHED, AND SMYTHE
Partnership Liquidation Schedule

	Cash	+	Other Assets	=	Accounts Payable	+	Mural, Capital	+	Lynched, Capital	+	Smythe, Capital

PROBLEM **A13-9**

Mural, Lynched, and Smythe

NAME
SECTION
DATE

1.

MURAL, LYNCHED, AND SMYTHE
Partnership Liquidation Schedule

	Cash	+	Other Assets	=	Accounts Payable	+	Mural, Capital	+	Lynched, Capital	+	Smythe, Capital

2.

MURAL, LYNCHED, AND SMYTHE
Partnership Liquidation Schedule

	Cash	+	Other Assets	=	Accounts Payable	+	Mural, Capital	+	Lynched, Capital	+	Smythe, Capital

PROBLEM **A13-9**

Mural, Lynched, and Smythe *(concluded)*

3.

MURAL, LYNCHED, AND SMYTHE
Partnership Liquidation Schedule

	Cash	+	Other Assets	=	Accounts Payable	+	Mural, Capital	+	Lynched, Capital	+	Smythe, Capital

PROBLEM **A14-1**

NAME
SECTION
DATE

Arcos Inc.

	General Journal			
		Post.		
Date	Account Titles and Explanation	Ref.	Debit	Credit
1990				

PROBLEM **A14-2**

Linn Company

NAME

SECTION

DATE

	General Journal			
		Post.		
Date	Account Titles and Explanation	Ref.	Debit	Credit
1991				

PROBLEM **A14-3**

Plaza Corp.

NAME
SECTION
DATE

Date	General Journal Account Titles and Explanation	Post. Ref.	Debit	Credit
1990				

PROBLEM **A14-4**

Eastech Inc.

NAME

SECTION

DATE

1.	Preferred	Common	Total

2.	Preferred	Common	Total

PROBLEM **A14-4**

Eastech Inc. *(concluded)*

3.	**Preferred**	**Common**	**Total**

PROBLEM **A14-5**

Caster Pools Inc.

NAME
SECTION
DATE

1.

Cash

Land

Preferred Stock

Common Stock

Stock Subscriptions Receivable

Organization Costs

Paid-In Capital in Excess of Par: Preferred

Common Stock Subscribed

PROBLEM **A14-5**

Caster Pools Inc. *(continued)*

Paid-In Capital in Excess of Par: Common

Donated Capital

Retained Earnings

Paid-In Capital from Treasury Stock

Treasury Stock

PROBLEM **A14-5**

Caster Pools Inc. *(concluded)*

NAME

SECTION

DATE

CASTER POOLS INC.
Stockholders' Equity
December 31, 1990

PROBLEM **A14-6**

Starr Inc.

NAME

SECTION

DATE

STARR INC. Stockholders' Equity December 31, 1990		

PROBLEM **B2-1**

Classic Pictures

NAME Suzanne Anderson

SECTION

DATE 6/3

1.

CLASSIC PICTURES
Income Statement
Month Ended May 31, 1990

Revenue:		
Consulting Revenue		5090 00
Expenses:		
Salaries Expense	2050 00	
Framing Expense	860 00	
Insurance Expense	750 00	
Rent Expense	400 00	
Utilities	120 00	
		4180 00
Net Income		910 00

2.

CLASSIC PICTURES
Statement of Owner's Equity
Month Ended May 31, 1990

Shelly, Capital 5/1/92		2500 00
Add: Net Income		910 00
Investment		500 00
Total		3910 00
Less: Withdrawal		300 00
Shelly, Capital 5/31/92		3610 00

PROBLEM **B2-2**

Costello Company

NAME Suzanne Anderson
SECTION
DATE 6/3

COSTELLO COMPANY
Balance Sheet
June 30, 1990

Assets		**Liabilities & Owner's Equity**	
Cash	5450 —		
Accts Rec	12330 —	**Liabilities:**	
Office Equip	17250 —	Notes Pay	10000 —
Delivery Truck	15400 —	Accts Pay	4260 —
Delivery Supplies on hand	1600 —	Salaries Pay	1770 —
Office Supplies on hand	1020 —		16030 —
		Owner's Equity:	
		Costello, Capital	37020 —
		Total Liabilities and	
Total Assets	53050	**Owner's Equity**	53050 —

PROBLEM **B2-3**

NAME
SECTION
DATE

Channey's Costumes

1.

CHANNEY'S COSTUMES
Financial Transaction Worksheet
Month of November, 1990

Trans-action	Cash	Accounts Receivable	Supplies on Hand	Costumes	Accounts Payable	Channey, Capital	Owner's Equity Explanation
Start							
a.							
b.							
c.							
d.							
e.							
f.							
g.							
h.							
i.							
j.							

2.

Revenue

Expenses

Net Income

PROBLEM **B2-4**

Lanchester Beauty Shop

NAME Suzanne Anderson
SECTION classwork
DATE 6/8

1.

LANCHESTER BEAUTY SHOP
Financial Transaction Worksheet
Month of July, 1990

Transaction	Cash	Accounts Receivable	Beauty Supplies on Hand	Beauty Equipment	Accounts Payable	Lanchester, Capital	Owner's Equity Explanation
			1900	2800		4700	
a.	1500					1500	
b.		370				370	
c.			425		425		
d.				850	850		
e.	930					930	
f.	(175)					(175)	
g.	(225)				(225)		
h.		590				590	
i.	(40)					(40)	
j.	(325)					(325)	
k.	(415)					(415)	
l.	250	(250)					
	1500	710	2325	3650	1050	7135	

PROBLEM **B2-4**

Lanchester Beauty Shop *(concluded)*

2.a.

LANCHESTER BEAUTY SHOP
Income Statement
Month Ended July 31, 1990

Revenue:		
Hairstyling Income		
		1890
Expenses:		
Repair Expense	175	
Wages	325	
Utilities	40	
Total Expenses		540
		1350
Net Income		

2.b.

LANCHESTER BEAUTY SHOP
Statement of Owner's Equity
Month Ended July 31, 1990

Lanchester, Capital July 1, 1990		4700
add:		
Investments		1500
Income		1350
Total		7550
Less Withdrawals		(415)
Lanchester, Capital July 31, 1990		7135

2.c.

LANCHESTER BEAUTY SHOP
Balance Sheet
July 31, 1990

Assets		**Liabilities & Owner's Equity**	
Cash	1500	**Liabilities:**	
Accts Rec	710	Accts Pay	1050
Beauty Supplies on hand	2325		
Beauty Equipment	3650	**Owner's Equity:**	
		Lanchester, Capital	7135
		Total Liabilities and	
Total Assets	8185	**Owner's Equity**	8185

PROBLEM **B2-5** Worksheet for parts 1 and 2 of this problem is at the back of this book.

NAME
SECTION
DATE

De Lacey Carpet-Cleaning Service *(concluded)*

3.a.

DE LACEY CARPET-CLEANING SERVICE
Income Statement
Month Ended January 31, 1990

Revenue:		
Expenses:		
Net Income		

3.b.

DE LACEY CARPET-CLEANING SERVICE
Statement of Owner's Equity
Month Ended January 31, 1990

3.c.

DE LACEY CARPET-CLEANING SERVICE
Balance Sheet
January 31, 1990

Assets		**Liabilities & Owner's Equity**	
		Liabilities:	
		Owner's Equity:	
		Total Liabilities and	
Total Assets		Owner's Equity	

PROBLEM **B2-6**

Victor Frankenstein, CPA

NAME Suzanne Gideon
SECTION
DATE 6/3

VICTOR FRANKENSTEIN, CPA
Income Statement
Year Ended December 31, 1990

Revenue:		272300 —
Auditing Fees Earned		
Expenses:		
Office Supplies Expense	19200 —	
Professional Development Expense	17300 —	
Rent Expense	10500 —	
Salaries Expense	147000 —	
Travel Expense	8200 —	
Utilities Expense	3600 —	
		205800 —
Net Income		66500 —

VICTOR FRANKENSTEIN, CPA
Statement of Owner's Equity
Year Ended December 31, 1990

Frankenstein, Capital Jan 1, 1990		261700 —
add: Net Income		66500 —
Investment		4400 —
Total		332600 —
Less: Withdrawals		33000 —
Frankenstein, Capital Dec. 31, 1990		299600 —

VICTOR FRANKENSTEIN, CPA
Balance Sheet
December 31, 1990

Assets		**Liabilities & Owner's Equity**	
Cash	23700 —		
Accts Rec	39600 —	**Liabilities:**	
Building	150000 —	Accts. Pay.	12700 —
Land	15000 —	Salaries Pay	6100 —
Notes Rec	12000 —	Total Liab	18800
Office Equip	72500 —		
Office Supplies on hand	5600 —	**Owner's Equity:**	299600 —
Total Assets	318400 —	**Total Liabilities and Owner's Equity**	318400

CHAPTER 2 DECISION PROBLEM

NAME

SECTION

DATE

McDraw Consulting Company

PROBLEM **B3-1**

Anderson Hanging Service

NAME

SECTION

DATE

1.

ANDERSON HANGING SERVICE
General Ledger T-Accounts

Cash

Accounts Receivable

Paperhanging Supplies on Hand

Prepaid Advertising

Truck

Notes Payable

Accounts Payable

Anderson, Capital

Anderson, Withdrawals

Paperhanging Fees Earned

Salary Expense

Rent Expense

Telephone Expense

Miscellaneous Expense

PROBLEM **B3-1**

Anderson Hanging Service *(concluded)*

2.

ANDERSON HANGING SERVICE
Trial Balance
February 28, 1990

PROBLEM **B3-2**

Abraham Gray, Attorney at Law

NAME
SECTION
DATE

1.		General Journal			
			Post.		
Date		Account Titles and Explanation	Ref.	Debit	Credit
1990					
Mar.					

PROBLEM **B3-2**

Abraham Gray, Attorney at Law *(continued)*

Date		General Journal Account Titles and Explanation	Post. Ref.	Debit	Credit
1990					
Mar.					

PROBLEM **B3-2**

NAME

SECTION

DATE

Abraham Gray, Attorney at Law *(continued)*

General Ledger

Date		Cash Explanation	Post. Ref.	Debit	Credit	Acct. No. 110 Balance
1990						
Mar.						

Date		Accounts Receivable Explanation	Post. Ref.	Debit	Credit	Acct. No. 120 Balance
1990						
Mar.						

Date		Office Supplies on Hand Explanation	Post. Ref.	Debit	Credit	Acct. No. 130 Balance
1990						
Mar.						

Date		Land Explanation	Post. Ref.	Debit	Credit	Acct. No. 140 Balance
1990						
Mar.						

Date		Building Explanation	Post. Ref.	Debit	Credit	Acct. No. 150 Balance
1990						
Mar.						

PROBLEM **B3-2**

Abraham Gray, Attorney at Law *(continued)*

Date	Office Equipment Explanation	Post. Ref.	Debit	Credit	Acct. No. 160 Balance
1990					
Mar.					

Date	Law Library Explanation	Post. Ref.	Debit	Credit	Acct. No. 170 Balance
1990					
Mar.					

Date	Accounts Payable Explanation	Post. Ref.	Debit	Credit	Acct. No. 210 Balance
1990					
Mar.					

Date	Mortgage Payable Explanation	Post. Ref.	Debit	Credit	Acct. No. 220 Balance
1990					
Mar.					

Date	Gray, Capital Explanation	Post. Ref.	Debit	Credit	Acct. No. 310 Balance
1990					
Mar.					

Date	Gray, Withdrawals Explanation	Post. Ref.	Debit	Credit	Acct. No. 320 Balance
1990					
Mar.					

PROBLEM **B3-2**

NAME
SECTION
DATE

Abraham Gray, Attorney at Law *(continued)*

Date	Legal Fees Earned Explanation	Post. Ref.	Debit	Credit	Acct. No. 410 Balance
1990					
Mar.					

Date	Salary Expense Explanation	Post. Ref.	Debit	Credit	Acct. No. 510 Balance
1990					
Mar.					

Date	Rent Expense Explanation	Post. Ref.	Debit	Credit	Acct. No. 520 Balance
1990					
Mar.					

Date	Telephone Expense Explanation	Post. Ref.	Debit	Credit	Acct. No. 530 Balance
1990					
Mar.					

Date	Professional Dues Expense Explanation	Post. Ref.	Debit	Credit	Acct. No. 540 Balance
1990					
Mar.					

PROBLEM **B3-2**

Abraham Gray, Attorney at Law *(concluded)*

3.

ABRAHAM GRAY, ATTORNEY AT LAW
Trial Balance
March 31, 1990

NAME
SECTION
DATE

PROBLEM B3-3

Diane's Repair Shoppe

Date		General Journal Account Titles and Explanation	Post. Ref.	Debit	Credit
1990					
Jan.					

Accounts Receivable

Accounts Payable

Cash

PROBLEM **B3-5**

Bristol Pirates

NAME
SECTION
DATE

2.		General Journal			
			Post.		
Date		Account Titles and Explanation	Ref.	Debit	Credit
1990					
May					

PROBLEM **B3-5**

Bristol Pirates *(continued)*

Date		General Journal Account Titles and Explanation	Post. Ref.	Debit	Credit
1990					
May					

PROBLEM **B3-5**

Bristol Pirates *(continued)*

NAME

SECTION

DATE

General Ledger

1. and 3.

Date		Cash Explanation	Post. Ref.	Debit	Credit	Acct. No. 110 Balance
1990						
May						

Date		Accounts Receivable Explanation	Post. Ref.	Debit	Credit	Acct. No. 120 Balance
1990						
May						

Date		Uniform Supplies on Hand Explanation	Post. Ref.	Debit	Credit	Acct. No. 130 Balance
1990						
May						

Date		Prepaid Insurance Explanation	Post. Ref.	Debit	Credit	Acct. No. 140 Balance
1990						
May						

PROBLEM **B3-5**

Bristol Pirates *(continued)*

Date		Land Explanation	Post. Ref.	Debit	Credit	Acct. No. 150 Balance
1990						
May						

Date		Sports Complex Explanation	Post. Ref.	Debit	Credit	Acct. No. 160 Balance
1990						
May						

Date		Training Equipment Explanation	Post. Ref.	Debit	Credit	Acct. No. 170 Balance
1990						
May						

Date		Player Contracts Explanation	Post. Ref.	Debit	Credit	Acct. No. 180 Balance
1990						
May						

Date		Notes Payable Explanation	Post. Ref.	Debit	Credit	Acct. No. 210 Balance
1990						
May						

PROBLEM **B3-5**

Bristol Pirates *(continued)*

NAME

SECTION

DATE

Date	Accounts Payable Explanation	Post. Ref.	Debit	Credit	Acct. No. 220 Balance
1990					
May					

Date	Mortgage Payable Explanation	Post. Ref.	Debit	Credit	Acct. No. 230 Balance
1990					
May					

Date	Lucy Dogger, Capital Explanation	Post. Ref.	Debit	Credit	Acct. No. 310 Balance
1990					
May					

Date	Lucy Dogger, Withdrawals Explanation	Post. Ref.	Debit	Credit	Acct. No. 320 Balance
1990					
May					

Date	Game Attendance Fees Earned Explanation	Post. Ref.	Debit	Credit	Acct. No. 410 Balance
1990					
May					

PROBLEM **B3-5**

Bristol Pirates *(continued)*

Date		Player Salaries Explanation	Post. Ref.	Debit	Credit	Acct. No. 510 Balance
1990						
May						

Date		Advertising Expense Explanation	Post. Ref.	Debit	Credit	Acct. No. 520 Balance
1990						
May						

Date		Travel Expense Explanation	Post. Ref.	Debit	Credit	Acct. No. 530 Balance
1990						
May						

Date		Laundry Expense Explanation	Post. Ref.	Debit	Credit	Acct. No. 540 Balance
1990						
May						

Date		Medical Expense Explanation	Post. Ref.	Debit	Credit	Acct. No. 550 Balance
1990						
May						

Date		Utilities Expense Explanation	Post. Ref.	Debit	Credit	Acct. No. 560 Balance
1990						
May						

PROBLEM **B3-5**

Bristol Pirates *(continued)*

NAME
SECTION
DATE

Date		Miscellaneous Expense Explanation	Post. Ref.	Debit	Credit	Acct. No. 570 Balance
1990						
May						

4.

BRISTOL PIRATES Trial Balance May 31, 1990		

PROBLEM **B3-5**

Bristol Pirates *(concluded)*

5.

BRISTOL PIRATES
Income Statement
Five Months Ended May 31, 1990

BRISTOL PIRATES
Statement of Owner's Equity
Five Months Ended May 31, 1990

BRISTOL PIRATES
Balance Sheet
May 31, 1990

Assets		Liabilities & Owner's Equity	

PROBLEM **B3-6**

Silver Treasure Shoppe

NAME

SECTION

DATE

SILVER TREASURE SHOPPE Trial Balance October 31, 1990		
Cash		
Accounts Receivable		
Office Supplies on Hand		
Display Equipment		
Delivery Truck		
Accounts Payable		
Silver, Capital		
Silver, Withdrawals		
Revenue Earned		
Salary Expense		
Rent Expense		
Telephone Expense		
Totals		

NAME
SECTION
DATE

CHAPTER 3 DECISION PROBLEM

Bristol Badboys

(not required) **General Journal**

Date	Account Titles and Explanation	Post. Ref.	Debit	Credit
1991				
Apr.				

BRISTOL BADBOYS
General Ledger T-Accounts

Cash

Accounts Receivable

Training Camp Equipment

Player Equipment

Notes Payable

Accounts Payable

Salaries Payable

Advertising Expense

Hawkins, Capital

Hawkins, Withdrawals

Admission Fees

Television Revenues

Salary Expense

Training Camp Expense

Cleaning Expenses

Rent Expense

NAME
SECTION
DATE

CHAPTER 3 DECISION PROBLEM

Bristol Badboys *(concluded)*

BRISTOL BADBOYS
Income Statement
Nine Months Ended December 31, 1991

BRISTOL BADBOYS
Statement of Owner's Equity
Nine Months Ended December 31, 1991

BRISTOL BADBOYS
Balance Sheet
December 31, 1991

Assets		Liabilities & Owner's Equity	

PROBLEM **B4-1**

NAME
SECTION
DATE

Edinburgh Equipment Company

1.	General Journal			
		Post.		
Date	Account Titles and Explanation	Ref.	Debit	Credit
1990				
a.				
July				
b.				
c.				
d.				
e.				
2.				
1990				
Aug.				

PROBLEM **B4-3**

NAME
SECTION
DATE

Jacobite Travel Agency

1.		General Journal			
			Post.		
Date		Account Titles and Explanation	Ref.	Debit	Credit
		Adjusting Entries			
1990					
a.					
Dec.					
b.					
c.					
d.					
e.					

General Ledger

			Post.			Acct. No. 110
Date		Cash	Ref.	Debit	Credit	Balance

			Post.			Acct. No. 120
Date		Accounts Receivable	Ref.	Debit	Credit	Balance

			Post.			Acct. No. 130
Date		Prepaid Rent	Ref.	Debit	Credit	Balance

PROBLEM **B4-3**

Jacobite Travel Agency *(continued)*

Date		Office Supplies on Hand	Post. Ref.	Debit	Credit	Acct. No. 140 Balance

Date		Furniture	Post. Ref.	Debit	Credit	Acct. No. 150 Balance

Date		Accum. Depr.: Furniture	Post. Ref.	Debit	Credit	Acct. No. 155 Balance

Date		Notes Payable	Post. Ref.	Debit	Credit	Acct. No. 210 Balance

Date		Interest Payable	Post. Ref.	Debit	Credit	Acct. No. 220 Balance

Date		Accounts Payable	Post. Ref.	Debit	Credit	Acct. No. 230 Balance

PROBLEM **B4-3**

NAME
SECTION
DATE

Jacobite Travel Agency *(continued)*

Date		Salaries Payable	Post. Ref.	Debit	Credit	Acct. No. 240 Balance
1990						
Dec.						

Date		Jacobite, Capital	Post. Ref.	Debit	Credit	Acct. No. 310 Balance
1990						

Date		Jacobite, Withdrawals	Post. Ref.	Debit	Credit	Acct. No. 320 Balance
1990						

Date		Travel Fees Earned	Post. Ref.	Debit	Credit	Acct. No. 410 Balance
1990						

Date		Salary Expense	Post. Ref.	Debit	Credit	Acct. No. 510 Balance
1990						
Dec.						

Date		Rent Expense	Post. Ref.	Debit	Credit	Acct. No. 520 Balance
1990						
Dec.						

PROBLEM **B4-3**

Jacobite Travel Agency *(continued)*

Date		Office Supplies Expense	Post. Ref.	Debit	Credit	Acct. No. 530 Balance
1990						
Dec.						

Date		Deprec. Expense: Furniture	Post. Ref.	Debit	Credit	Acct. No. 540 Balance

Date		Interest Expense	Post. Ref.	Debit	Credit	Acct. No. 550 Balance

Date		Miscellaneous Expense	Post. Ref.	Debit	Credit	Acct. No. 560 Balance

PROBLEM **B4-3**

NAME
SECTION
DATE

Jacobite Travel Agency *(concluded)*

JACOBITE TRAVEL AGENCY Adjusted Trial Balance December 31, 1990		
Cash		
Accounts Receivable		
Prepaid Rent		
Office Supplies on Hand		
Furniture		
Accumulated Depreciation: Furniture		
Notes Payable		
Interest Payable		
Accounts Payable		
Salaries Payable		
Jacobite, Capital		
Jacobite, Withdrawals		
Travel Fees Earned		
Salary Expense		
Rent Expense		
Office Supplies Expense		
Depreciation Expense: Furniture		
Interest Expense		
Miscellaneous Expense		
Totals		

PROBLEM **B4-4**

NAME
SECTION
DATE

John Breck Maccoll School for the Gifted

1. General Journal

Date	Account Titles and Explanation	Post. Ref.	Debit	Credit
1990				
a.				
Dec.				
b.				
c.				
d.				
e.				

General Ledger

2.

Date	Cash	Post. Ref.	Debit	Credit	Acct. No. Balance

Date	Notes Receivable	Post. Ref.	Debit	Credit	Acct. No. Balance

Date	Interest Receivable	Post. Ref.	Debit	Credit	Acct. No. Balance

PROBLEM **B4-4**

John Breck Maccoll School for the Gifted *(continued)*

Date		Accounts Receivable	Post. Ref.	Debit	Credit	Acct. No. Balance

Date		Prepaid Advertising	Post. Ref.	Debit	Credit	Acct. No. Balance

Date		School Supplies on Hand	Post. Ref.	Debit	Credit	Acct. No. Balance

Date		Land	Post. Ref.	Debit	Credit	Acct. No. Balance

Date		School Building	Post. Ref.	Debit	Credit	Acct. No. Balance

Date		Accum. Depr.: School Building	Post. Ref.	Debit	Credit	Acct. No. Balance

PROBLEM **B4-4**

NAME

SECTION

DATE

John Breck Maccoll School for the Gifted *(continued)*

Date		School Equipment	Post. Ref.	Debit	Credit	Acct. No. Balance

Date		Accum. Depr.: School Equip.	Post. Ref.	Debit	Credit	Acct. No. Balance

Date		Accounts Payable	Post. Ref.	Debit	Credit	Acct. No. Balance

Date		Salaries Payable	Post. Ref.	Debit	Credit	Acct. No. Balance

Date		Unearned Tuition Fees	Post. Ref.	Debit	Credit	Acct. No. Balance

Date		Maccoll, Capital	Post. Ref.	Debit	Credit	Acct. No. Balance

PROBLEM **B4-4**

John Breck Maccoll School for the Gifted *(continued)*

Date		Maccoll, Withdrawals	Post. Ref.	Debit	Credit	Acct. No. Balance

Date		Tuition Fees Earned	Post. Ref.	Debit	Credit	Acct. No. Balance

Date		Interest Income	Post. Ref.	Debit	Credit	Acct. No. Balance

Date		Salary Expense	Post. Ref.	Debit	Credit	Acct. No. Balance

Date		School Supplies Expense	Post. Ref.	Debit	Credit	Acct. No. Balance

PROBLEM **B4-4**

NAME
SECTION
DATE

John Breck Maccoll School for the Gifted *(continued)*

Date		Deprec. Expense: School Bldg.	Post. Ref.	Debit	Credit	Acct. No. Balance

Date		Deprec. Expense: School Equip.	Post. Ref.	Debit	Credit	Acct. No. Balance

Date		Repairs Expense	Post. Ref.	Debit	Credit	Acct. No. Balance

Date		Miscellaneous Expense	Post. Ref.	Debit	Credit	Acct. No. Balance

PROBLEM **B4-4**

John Breck Maccoll School for the Gifted *(continued)*

3. JOHN BRECK MACCOLL SCHOOL FOR THE GIFTED
Adjusted Trial Balance
December 31, 1990

Cash		
Notes Receivable		
Interest Receivable		
Accounts Receivable		
Prepaid Advertising		
School Supplies on Hand		
Land		
School Building		
Accumulated Depreciation: School Building		
School Equipment		
Accumulated Depreciation: School Equipment		
Accounts Payable		
Salaries Payable		
Unearned Tuition Fees		
Maccoll, Capital		
Maccoll, Withdrawals		
Tuition Fees Earned		
Interest Income		
Salary Expense		
School Supplies Expense		
Depreciation Expense: School Building		
Depreciation Expense: School Equipment		
Repairs Expense		
Miscellaneous Expense		
Totals		

4. JOHN BRECK MACCOLL SCHOOL FOR THE GIFTED
Income Statement
Year Ended December 31, 1990

Revenue:		
Revenue		
Interest Income		
Total Revenue		
Expenses:		
Salary Expense		
School Supplies Expense		
Depreciation Expense: School Building		
Depreciation Expense: School Equipment		
Repairs Expense		
Miscellaneous Expense		
Total Expenses		
Net Income		

PROBLEM **B4-4**

NAME
SECTION
DATE

John Breck Maccoll School for the Gifted *(concluded)*

JOHN BRECK MACCOLL SCHOOL FOR THE GIFTED Statement of Owner's Equity Year Ended December 31, 1990		
Maccoll, Capital, Jan. 1, 1990		
Add: Net Income		
Total		
Less: Withdrawal		
Maccoll, Capital Dec. 31, 1990		

JOHN BRECK MACCOLL SCHOOL FOR THE GIFTED Balance Sheet December 31, 1990			
Assets		**Liabilities & Owner's Equity**	
Current Assets:		Liabilities:	
Cash		Current Liabilities:	
Notes Receivable		Accounts Payable	
Interest Receivable		Salaries Payable	
Accounts Receivable		Unearned Tuition Fees	
Prepaid Advertising		Total Current Liabilities	
School Supplies on Hand			
Total Current Assets		Owner's Equity:	
		Maccoll, Capital	
Property, Plant, and Equipment:			
Land			
School Bldg.			
Less: Acc. Depr.			
School Equip.			
Less: Acc. Depr.			
Total Property,			
Plant, and Equipment			
		Total Liabilities and	
Total Assets		Owner's Equity	

PROBLEM **B4-5**

House of Stuart

NAME
SECTION
DATE

Date		General Journal Account Titles and Explanation	Post. Ref.	Debit	Credit
1990					
Dec.	31				
	31				
	31				
	31				
	31				

PROBLEM **B4-6**

NAME
SECTION
DATE

Bonnie Prince Charlie Company

BONNIE PRINCE CHARLIE COMPANY
Balance Sheet
December 31, 1990

Assets		**Liabilities & Owner's Equity**	
Current Assets:		**Liabilities:**	
		Current Liabilities:	
		Long-Term Liabilities:	
Investments:			
		Owner's Equity:	
Property, Plant, and Equipment:			
Intangibles:			
		Total Liabilities	
Total Assets		**and Owner's Equity**	

CHAPTER 4 DECISION PROBLEM

Covenant Cargo

NAME
SECTION
DATE

1.

COVENANT CARGO
Income Statement: (Cash-Basis)
For the Year Ended December 31, 1990

	1989	1990	1991
Revenues			
Expenses:			
Salaries			
Repairs Expense			
Total Expenses			
Net Income/(loss)			

2.

COVENANT CARGO
Income Statement: (Accrual-Basis)
For the Year Ended December 31, 1990

	1989	1990	1991
Revenues			
Expenses:			
Salaries			
Repairs Expense			
Total Expenses			
Net Income			

3.

PROBLEM **B5-2**

NAME
SECTION
DATE

Allyson Martinez, Attorney at Law

General Journal				
Date	Account Titles and Explanation	Post. Ref.	Debit	Credit
	Closing Entries			

PROBLEM **B5-4**

Newcomen Detective Agency

NAME
SECTION
DATE

	General Journal			Page 1
Date	Account Titles and Explanation	Post. Ref.	Debit	Credit

PROBLEM **B5-4**

Newcomen Detective Agency *(continued)*

General Journal

Date	Account Titles and Explanation	Post. Ref.	Debit	Credit

Adjusting Entries

PROBLEM **B5-4**

NAME
SECTION
DATE

Newcomen Detective Agency *(continued)*

General Journal

Date		Account Titles and Explanation	Post. Ref.	Debit	Credit
		Closing Entries			
		Reversing Entries			

PROBLEM **B5-4**

Newcomen Detective Agency *(continued)*

General Ledger

Date	Cash	Post. Ref.	Debit	Credit	Acct. No. 110 Balance

Date	Accounts Receivable	Post. Ref.	Debit	Credit	Acct. No. 120 Balance

Date	Office Supplies on Hand	Post. Ref.	Debit	Credit	Acct. No. 130 Balance

Date	Prepaid Rent	Post. Ref.	Debit	Credit	Acct. No. 140 Balance

Date	Prepaid Advertising	Post. Ref.	Debit	Credit	Acct. No. 150 Balance

PROBLEM **B5-4**

NAME

SECTION

DATE

Newcomen Detective Agency *(continued)*

Date	Office Equipment	Post. Ref.	Debit	Credit	Acct. No. 160 Balance

Date	Accumulated Depreciation	Post. Ref.	Debit	Credit	Acct. No. 165 Balance

Date	Accounts Payable	Post. Ref.	Debit	Credit	Acct. No. 210 Balance

Date	Salaries Payable	Post. Ref.	Debit	Credit	Acct. No. 220 Balance

Date	Unearned Investigation Fees	Post. Ref.	Debit	Credit	Acct. No. 230 Balance

Date	Interest Payable	Post. Ref.	Debit	Credit	Acct. No. 240 Balance

PROBLEM **B5-4**

Newcomen Detective Agency *(continued)*

Date		Note Payable	Post. Ref.	Debit	Credit	Acct. No. 250 Balance

Date		Newcomen, Capital	Post. Ref.	Debit	Credit	Acct. No. 310 Balance

Date		Newcomen, Withdrawals	Post. Ref.	Debit	Credit	Acct. No. 320 Balance

Date		Expense and Revenue Summary	Post. Ref.	Debit	Credit	Acct. No. 330 Balance

Date		Investigation Fees Earned	Post. Ref.	Debit	Credit	Acct. No. 410 Balance

PROBLEM **B5-4**

NAME
SECTION
DATE

Newcomen Detective Agency *(continued)*

Date	Salary Expense	Post. Ref.	Debit	Credit	Acct. No. 510 Balance

Date	Office Supplies Expense	Post. Ref.	Debit	Credit	Acct. No. 520 Balance

Date	Rent Expense	Post. Ref.	Debit	Credit	Acct. No. 530 Balance

Date	Advertising Expense	Post. Ref.	Debit	Credit	Acct. No. 540 Balance

Date	Depreciation Expense	Post. Ref.	Debit	Credit	Acct. No. 550 Balance

PROBLEM **B5-4**

Newcomen Detective Agency *(continued)*

Date	Repairs Expense	Post. Ref.	Debit	Credit	Acct. No. 560 Balance

Date	Telephone Expense	Post. Ref.	Debit	Credit	Acct. No. 570 Balance

Date	Travel Expense	Post. Ref.	Debit	Credit	Acct. No. 580 Balance

Date	Interest Expense	Post. Ref.	Debit	Credit	Acct. No. 590 Balance

PROBLEM **B5-4**

Worksheet for this problem is at the back of this book.

NAME
SECTION
DATE

Newcomen Detective Agency *(continued)*

NEWCOMEN DETECTIVE AGENCY
Income Statement
Month Ended July 31, 1990

NEWCOMEN DETECTIVE AGENCY
Statement of Owner's Equity
Month Ended July 31, 1990

PROBLEM **B5-4**

Newcomen Detective Agency *(concluded)*

NEWCOMEN DETECTIVE AGENCY Balance Sheet July 31, 1990			
Assets		**Liabilities & Owner's Equity**	

NEWCOMEN DETECTIVE AGENCY Post-Closing Trial Balance July 31, 1990		

CHAPTER 5 DECISION PROBLEM

Worksheet for problem B5-5 is at the back of this book.

NAME
SECTION
DATE

Dr. Jekyll Research Laboratory

DR. JEKYLL RESEARCH LABORATORY Income Statement	1985–1989	1989

DR. JEKYLL RESEARCH LABORATORY Statement of Owner's Equity For the Five Years Ending December 31, 1989		

Dr. Jekyll Research Laboratory *(concluded)*

DR. JEKYLL RESEARCH LABORATORY			
Balance Sheet			
December 31, 1989			
Assets		**Liabilities & Owner's Equity**	

PROBLEM **B6-1**

Portland Company

NAME
SECTION
DATE

PORTLAND COMPANY
Income Statement
Year Ended December 31, 1990

PROBLEM **B6-2**

NAME
SECTION
DATE

The Maine Sales Company

1.

Date		THE MAINE SALES COMPANY General Journal Account Titles and Explanation	Post. Ref.	Debit	Credit
1990					
May					

PROBLEM **B6-2**

The Maine Sales Company *(concluded)*

2.	ORENO SUPPLY COMPANY			
	General Journal	Post.		
Date	**Account Titles and Explanation**	**Ref.**	**Debit**	**Credit**
1990				
May				

PROBLEM **B6-3**

Worksheet for this problem is at the back of this book.

NAME
SECTION
DATE

Jordan Company *(concluded)*

2.		General Journal			
Date		Account Titles and Explanation	Post. Ref.	Debit	Credit
		Closing Entries			
1990					
Dec.					

PROBLEM **B6-4**

Worksheet for this problem is at the back of this book.

NAME

SECTION

DATE

Kennebunk Company *(continued)*

KENNEBUNK COMPANY
Income Statement
Year Ended December 31, 1990

KENNEBUNK COMPANY
Statement of Changes in Owner's Equity
Year Ended December 31, 1990

PROBLEM **B6-4**

Kennebunk Company *(continued)*

KENNEBUNK COMPANY Balance Sheet December 31, 1990			
Assets		**Liabilities & Owner's Equity**	

PROBLEM **B6-4**

Kennebunk Company *(continued)*

NAME

SECTION

DATE

Date		General Journal Account Titles and Explanation	Post. Ref.	Debit	Credit
		Adjusting Entries			
1990					
Dec.					

PROBLEM **B6-4**

Kennebunk Company *(concluded)*

Date		General Journal Account Titles and Explanation	Post. Ref.	Debit	Credit
1990					
Dec.					

PROBLEM **B6-5**

The Bigelow Company

NAME
SECTION
DATE

Date	General Journal Account Titles and Explanation	Post. Ref.	Debit	Credit
1990				
Dec.				

PROBLEM **B6-5**

The Bigelow Company *(continued)*

General Journal

Date		Account Titles and Explanation	Post. Ref.	Debit	Credit
1990					
Dec.					

PROBLEM **B6-5**

NAME

SECTION

DATE

The Bigelow Company *(continued)*

General Journal				
Date	Account Titles and Explanation	Post. Ref.	Debit	Credit
1990				
Dec.				
	Adjusting Entries			

PROBLEM **B6-5**

The Bigelow Company *(continued)*

General Journal

Date		Account Titles and Explanation	Post. Ref.	Debit	Credit
1990					
Dec.					
		Closing Entries			

PROBLEM **B6-5**

Worksheet for this problem is at the back of this book.

NAME
SECTION
DATE

The Bigelow Company *(continued)*

General Ledger

Date	Cash	Post. Ref.	Debit	Credit	Acct. No. 110 Balance
1990					
Dec.					

Date	Accounts Receivable	Post. Ref.	Debit	Credit	Acct. No. 120 Balance
1990					
Dec.					

Date	Merchandise Inventory	Post. Ref.	Debit	Credit	Acct. No. 130 Balance
1990					
Dec.					

Date	Office Supplies on Hand	Post. Ref.	Debit	Credit	Acct. No. 140 Balance
1990					
Dec.					

PROBLEM **B6-5**

The Bigelow Company *(continued)*

Date		Prepaid Insurance	Post. Ref.	Debit	Credit	Acct. No. 150 Balance
1990						
Dec.						

Date		Land	Post. Ref.	Debit	Credit	Acct. No. 160 Balance
1990						
Dec.						

Date		Building	Post. Ref.	Debit	Credit	Acct. No. 170 Balance
1990						
Dec.						

Date		Accumulated Depreciation: Building	Post. Ref.	Debit	Credit	Acct. No. 175 Balance
1990						
Dec.						

Date		Office Equipment	Post. Ref.	Debit	Credit	Acct. No. 180 Balance
1990						
Dec.						

Date		Accumulated Depreciation: Office Equipment	Post. Ref.	Debit	Credit	Acct. No. 185 Balance
1990						
Dec.						

PROBLEM **B6-5**

NAME
SECTION
DATE

The Bigelow Company *(continued)*

Date		Accounts Payable	Post. Ref.	Debit	Credit	Acct. No. 210 Balance
1990						
Dec.						

Date		Salaries Payable	Post. Ref.	Debit	Credit	Acct. No. 220 Balance
1990						
Dec.						

Date		Mortgage Payable	Post. Ref.	Debit	Credit	Acct. No. 230 Balance
1990						
Dec.						

Date		Bigelow, Capital	Post. Ref.	Debit	Credit	Acct. No. 310 Balance
1990						
Dec.						

Date		Bigelow, Withdrawals	Post. Ref.	Debit	Credit	Acct. No. 320 Balance
1990						
Dec.						

PROBLEM **B6-5**

The Bigelow Company *(continued)*

Date		Expense and Revenue Summary	Post. Ref.	Debit	Credit	Acct. No. 330 Balance
1990						
Dec.						

Date		Sales	Post. Ref.	Debit	Credit	Acct. No. 410 Balance
1990						
Dec.						

Date		Sales Returns and Allowances	Post. Ref.	Debit	Credit	Acct. No. 420 Balance
1990						
Dec.						

Date		Sales Discounts	Post. Ref.	Debit	Credit	Acct. No. 430 Balance
1990						
Dec.						

Date		Purchases	Post. Ref.	Debit	Credit	Acct. No. 510 Balance
1990						
Dec.						

Date		Purchases Returns and Allowances	Post. Ref.	Debit	Credit	Acct. No. 520 Balance
1990						
Dec.						

PROBLEM **B6-5**

NAME
SECTION
DATE

The Bigelow Company *(continued)*

Date		Purchases Discounts	Post. Ref.	Debit	Credit	Acct. No. 530 Balance
1990						
Dec.						

Date		Freight-In	Post. Ref.	Debit	Credit	Acct. No. 540 Balance
1990						
Dec.						

Date		Salary Expense	Post. Ref.	Debit	Credit	Acct. No. 610 Balance
1990						
Dec.						

Date		Office Supplies Expense	Post. Ref.	Debit	Credit	Acct. No. 620 Balance
1990						
Dec.						

Date		Insurance Expense	Post. Ref.	Debit	Credit	Acct. No. 630 Balance
1990						
Dec.						

Date		Depreciation Expense: Building	Post. Ref.	Debit	Credit	Acct. No. 640 Balance
1990						
Dec.						

PROBLEM **B6-5**

The Bigelow Company *(continued)*

Date		Depreciation Expense: Office Equipment	Post. Ref.	Debit	Credit	Acct. No. 650 Balance
1990						
Dec.						

Date		Delivery Expense	Post. Ref.	Debit	Credit	Acct. No. 660 Balance
1990						
Dec.						

Date		Entertainment Expense	Post. Ref.	Debit	Credit	Acct. No. 670 Balance
1990						
Dec.						

Date		Repairs Expense	Post. Ref.	Debit	Credit	Acct. No. 680 Balance
1990						
Dec.						

Date		Interest Expense	Post. Ref.	Debit	Credit	Acct. No. 690 Balance
1990						
Dec.						

Date			Post. Ref.	Debit	Credit	Acct. No. Balance

PROBLEM **B6-5**

The Bigelow Company *(continued)*

NAME
SECTION
DATE

THE BIGELOW COMPANY
Income Statement
Month Ended December 31, 1990

THE BIGELOW COMPANY
Statement of Changes in Owner's Equity
Year Ended December 31, 1990

PROBLEM **B6-5**

The Bigelow Company *(concluded)*

THE BIGELOW COMPANY
Balance Sheet
December 31, 1990

Assets		Liabilities & Owner's Equity	

CHAPTER 6 DECISION PROBLEM

The Austin Division

1.

2.

The Austin Division *(concluded)*

3.

PROBLEM **B7-1**

The Nittany Lion

NAME
SECTION
DATE

PROBLEM **B7-2**

Southeast Homes, Inc.

NAME

SECTION

DATE

PROBLEM **B7-3**

Raft Company

NAME
SECTION
DATE

1.

	Sales Journal			Page 1
Date	Account Debited	Invoice Number	Post. Ref.	Amount
1990				
Feb.				

	Purchases Journal			Page 2
Date	Account Credited	Invoice Date	Post. Ref.	Amount
1990				
Feb.				

	General Journal			Page 3
Date	Account Titles and Explanation	Post. Ref.	Debit	Credit
1990				
Feb.				

PROBLEM **B7-3**

Raft Company *(continued)*

General Ledger

2.

Date	Accounts Receivable Explanation	Post. Ref.	Debit	Credit	Acct. No. 120 Balance
1990					
Feb.					

Date	Accounts Payable Explanation	Post. Ref.	Debit	Credit	Acct. No. 210 Balance
1990					
Feb.					

Date	Sales Explanation	Post. Ref.	Debit	Credit	Acct. No. 410 Balance
1990					
Feb.					

Date	Sales Returns and Allowances Explanation	Post. Ref.	Debit	Credit	Acct. No. 420 Balance
1990					
Feb.					

Date	Purchases Explanation	Post. Ref.	Debit	Credit	Acct. No. 510 Balance
1990					
Feb.					

Date	Purchases Returns and Allow. Explanation	Post. Ref.	Debit	Credit	Acct. No. 520 Balance
1990					
Feb.					

PROBLEM **B7-3**

Raft Company *(continued)*

NAME

SECTION

DATE

Accounts Receivable Ledger

Date		Baker, J. Explanation	Post. Ref.	Debit	Credit	Balance
1990						
Feb.						

Date		Columbus, C. Explanation	Post. Ref.	Debit	Credit	Balance
1990						
Feb.						

Date		Joe, I. Explanation	Post. Ref.	Debit	Credit	Balance
1990						
Feb.						

Date		Joplin, J. Explanation	Post. Ref.	Debit	Credit	Balance
1990						
Feb.						

PROBLEM **B7-3**

Raft Company *(continued)*

Accounts Payable Ledger

Date		Cadiff Hill Company Explanation	Post. Ref.	Debit	Credit	Balance
1990						
Feb.						

Date		Finn Company Explanation	Post. Ref.	Debit	Credit	Balance
1990						
Feb.						

Date		Sawyer Company Explanation	Post. Ref.	Debit	Credit	Balance
1990						
Feb.						

Date		Walters, Ltd. Explanation	Post. Ref.	Debit	Credit	Balance
1990						
Feb.						

PROBLEM **B7-3**

NAME
SECTION
DATE

Raft Company *(concluded)*

3.

RAFT COMPANY Schedule of Accounts Receivable February 28, 1990	
Baker, J.	
Columbus, C.	
Joe, I.	
Joplin, J.	
Total	

RAFT COMPANY Schedule of Accounts Payable February 28, 1990	
Cadiff Hill Company	
Finn Company	
Sawyer Company	
Walters, Ltd.	
Total	

PROBLEM **B7-4**

DeVeto Company

NAME
SECTION
DATE

Cash Receipts Journal

Date	Account Credited	Post. Ref.	Sundry Accounts Credit	Accounts Receivable Credit	Sales Credit	Sales Discounts Debit	Cash Debit	
1990								
Mar.								

PROBLEM **B7-4**

DeVeto Company *(concluded)*

Cash Payments Journal

Date	Check Number	Account Debited	Post. Ref.	Sundry Accounts Debit	Accounts Payable Debit	Purchases Debit	Purchase Discounts Credit	Cash Credit
1990								
Mar.								

PROBLEM **B7-5**

Missouri Company

NAME
SECTION
DATE

	Sales Journal			Page 23
Date	**Account Debited**	**Invoice Number**	**Post. Ref.**	**Amount**
1990				
Apr.				

	General Journal			
Date	**Account Titles and Explanation**	**Post. Ref.**	**Debit**	**Credit**
1990				
Apr.				

PROBLEM **B7-5**

Missouri Company *(continued)*

Cash Receipts Journal

Date	Account Credited	Post. Ref.	Sundry Accounts Credit	Accounts Receivable Credit	Sales Credit	Sales Discounts Debit	Cash Debit	
1990								
Apr.								

PROBLEM **B7-5**

NAME

SECTION

DATE

Missouri Company *(continued)*

General Ledger

Date	Cash Explanation	Post. Ref.	Debit	Credit	Acct. No. 110 Balance
1990					
Apr.					

Date	Accounts Receivable Explanation	Post. Ref.	Debit	Credit	Acct. No. 120 Balance
1990					
Apr.					

Date	Notes Payable Explanation	Post. Ref.	Debit	Credit	Acct. No. 210 Balance
1990					
Apr.					

Date	Wilder, Capital Explanation	Post. Ref.	Debit	Credit	Acct. No. 310 Balance
1990					
Apr.					

PROBLEM **B7-5**

Missouri Company *(continued)*

Date		Sales Explanation	Post. Ref.	Debit	Credit	Acct. No. 410 Balance
1990						
Apr.						

Date		Sales Returns and Allowances Explanation	Post. Ref.	Debit	Credit	Acct. No. 420 Balance
1990						
Apr.						

Date		Sales Discounts Explanation	Post. Ref.	Debit	Credit	Acct. No. 430 Balance
1990						
Apr.						

Date		Explanation	Post. Ref.	Debit	Credit	Acct. No. Balance

PROBLEM **B7-5**

NAME
SECTION
DATE

Missouri Company *(concluded)*

Accounts Receivable Ledger

Date	Anderson, A. Explanation	Post. Ref.	Debit	Credit	Balance
1990					
Apr.					

Date	Brown, B. Explanation	Post. Ref.	Debit	Credit	Balance
1990					
Apr.					

Date	Cowen, C. Explanation	Post. Ref.	Debit	Credit	Balance
1990					
Apr.					

Date	Spade, S. Explanation	Post. Ref.	Debit	Credit	Balance
1990					
Apr.					

Date	Thompson, T. Explanation	Post. Ref.	Debit	Credit	Balance
1990					
Apr.					

MISSOURI COMPANY Schedule of Accounts Receivable April 30, 1990	
Cowen, C.	
Spade, S.	
Total	

PROBLEM **B7-6**

NAME
SECTION
DATE

Cardiff Company

	Purchases Journal			Page 22
		Invoice	Post.	
Date	Account Credited	Date	Ref.	Amount
1990				
May				

	General Journal			Page 16
		Post.		
Date	Account Titles and Explanation	Ref.	Debit	Credit
1990				
May				

PROBLEM **B7-6**

Cardiff Company *(continued)*

Cash Payments Journal

Date	Check Number	Account Debited	Post. Ref.	Sundry Accounts Debit	Accounts Payable Debit	Purchases Debit	Purchase Discounts Credit	Cash Credit
1990								
May								

PROBLEM **B7-6**

NAME
SECTION
DATE

Cardiff Company *(continued)*

General Ledger

Date	Cash Explanation	Post. Ref.	Debit	Credit	Acct. No. 110 Balance
1990					
May					

Date	Accounts Payable Explanation	Post. Ref.	Debit	Credit	Acct. No. 210 Balance
1990					
May					

Date	Cardiff, Withdrawals Explanation	Post. Ref.	Debit	Credit	Acct. No. 320 Balance
1990					
May					

Date	Purchases Explanation	Post. Ref.	Debit	Credit	Acct. No. 510 Balance
1990					
May					

PROBLEM **B7-6**

Cardiff Company *(continued)*

Date		Purchases Returns and Allow. Explanation	Post. Ref.	Debit	Credit	Acct. No. 520 Balance
1990						
May						

Date		Purchases Discounts Explanation	Post. Ref.	Debit	Credit	Acct. No. 530 Balance
1990						
May						

Date		Freight-In Explanation	Post. Ref.	Debit	Credit	Acct. No. 540 Balance
1990						
May						

Date		Salary Expense Explanation	Post. Ref.	Debit	Credit	Acct. No. 610 Balance
1990						
May						

Date		Insurance Expense Explanation	Post. Ref.	Debit	Credit	Acct. No. 620 Balance
1990						
May						

PROBLEM **B7-6**

Cardiff Company *(concluded)*

NAME
SECTION
DATE

Accounts Payable Ledger

Date		Central States Supply Company Explanation	Post. Ref.	Debit	Credit	Balance
1990						
May						

Date		Jackson Company Explanation	Post. Ref.	Debit	Credit	Balance
1990						
May						

Date		Jones Company Explanation	Post. Ref.	Debit	Credit	Balance
1990						
May						

Date		St. Louis Company Explanation	Post. Ref.	Debit	Credit	Balance
1990						
May						

Date		Tyler Company Explanation	Post. Ref.	Debit	Credit	Balance
1990						
May						

CARDIFF COMPANY Schedule of Accounts Payable May 31, 1990	
Jackson Company	
Jones Company	
Tyler Company	
Total	

PROBLEM **B7-7**

Tom Finn Retail Store

NAME
SECTION
DATE

2.

	Sales Journal			Page 8
Date	Account Debited	Invoice Number	Post. Ref.	Amount
1990				
June				

	Purchases Journal			Page 9
Date	Account Credited	Invoice Date	Post. Ref.	Amount
1990				
June				

PROBLEM **B7-7**

Tom Finn Retail Store *(continued)*

Cash Receipts Journal

Page 15

Date	Account Credited	Post. Ref.	Sundry Accounts Credit	Accounts Receivable Credit	Sales Credit	Sales Discounts Debit	Cash Debit	
1990								
June								

Cash Payments Journal

Page 17

Date	Check Number	Account Debited	Post. Ref.	Sundry Accounts Debit	Accounts Payable Debit	Purchases Debit	Purchase Discounts Credit	Cash Credit
1990								
June								

PROBLEM **B7-7**

NAME
SECTION
DATE

Tom Finn Retail Store *(continued)*

General Journal				Page 11
Date	**Account Titles and Explanation**	**Post. Ref.**	**Debit**	**Credit**
1990				
June				

8. General Journal				
Date	**Account Titles and Explanation**	**Post. Ref.**	**Debit**	**Credit**
	Adjusting Entries			
1990				
June				

PROBLEM **B7-7**

Tom Finn Retail Store *(continued)*

Date	General Journal Account Titles and Explanation	Post. Ref.	Debit	Credit
1990				
June				

PROBLEM **B7-7**

Worksheet for this problem is at the back of this book.

NAME

SECTION

DATE

Tom Finn Retail Store *(continued)*

General Ledger

1. and 3.

Date		Cash Explanation	Post. Ref.	Debit	Credit	Acct. No. 110 Balance
1990						
June						

Date		Accounts Receivable Explanation	Post. Ref.	Debit	Credit	Acct. No. 120 Balance
1990						
June						

Date		Merchandise Inventory Explanation	Post. Ref.	Debit	Credit	Acct. No. 130 Balance
1990						
June						

Date		Prepaid Insurance Explanation	Post. Ref.	Debit	Credit	Acct. No. 140 Balance
1990						
June						

Date		Office Supplies on Hand Explanation	Post. Ref.	Debit	Credit	Acct. No. 150 Balance
1990						
June						

Date		Office Equipment Explanation	Post. Ref.	Debit	Credit	Acct. No. 160 Balance
1990						
June						

PROBLEM **B7-7**

Tom Finn Retail Store *(continued)*

Date	Accumulated Depreciation Explanation	Post. Ref.	Debit	Credit	Acct. No. 165 Balance
1990					
June					

Date	Notes Payable Explanation	Post. Ref.	Debit	Credit	Acct. No. 210 Balance
1990					
June					

Date	Accounts Payable Explanation	Post. Ref.	Debit	Credit	Acct. No. 220 Balance
1990					
June					

Date	Salaries Payable Explanation	Post. Ref.	Debit	Credit	Acct. No. 230 Balance
1990					
June					

Date	Finn, Capital Explanation	Post. Ref.	Debit	Credit	Acct. No. 310 Balance
1990					
June					

Date	Finn, Withdrawals Explanation	Post. Ref.	Debit	Credit	Acct. No. 320 Balance
1990					
June					

PROBLEM **B7-7**

NAME
SECTION
DATE

Tom Finn Retail Store *(continued)*

Date		Expense and Revenue Summary Explanation	Post. Ref.	Debit	Credit	Acct. No. 330 Balance
1990						
June						

Date		Sales Explanation	Post. Ref.	Debit	Credit	Acct. No. 410 Balance
1990						
June						

Date		Sales Returns and Allowances Explanation	Post. Ref.	Debit	Credit	Acct. No. 420 Balance
1990						
June						

Date		Sales Discounts Explanation	Post. Ref.	Debit	Credit	Acct. No. 430 Balance
1990						
June						

Date		Purchases Explanation	Post. Ref.	Debit	Credit	Acct. No. 510 Balance
1990						
June						

Date		Purchases Returns and Allow. Explanation	Post. Ref.	Debit	Credit	Acct. No. 520 Balance
1990						
June						

PROBLEM **B7-7**

Tom Finn Retail Store *(continued)*

Date		Purchases Discounts Explanation	Post. Ref.	Debit	Credit	Acct. No. 530 Balance
1990						
June						

Date		Freight-In Explanation	Post. Ref.	Debit	Credit	Acct. No. 540 Balance
1990						
June						

Date		Salary Expense Explanation	Post. Ref.	Debit	Credit	Acct. No. 610 Balance
1990						
June						

Date		Insurance Expense Explanation	Post. Ref.	Debit	Credit	Acct. No. 620 Balance
1990						
June						

Date		Office Supplies Expense Explanation	Post. Ref.	Debit	Credit	Acct. No. 630 Balance
1990						
June						

Date		Depreciation Expense Explanation	Post. Ref.	Debit	Credit	Acct. No. 640 Balance
1990						
June						

PROBLEM **B7-7**

NAME
SECTION
DATE

Tom Finn Retail Store *(continued)*

Date	Interest Expense Explanation	Post. Ref.	Debit	Credit	Acct. No. 650 Balance
1990					
June					

Accounts Receivable Subsidiary Ledger

Date	Barnes, B. Explanation	Post. Ref.	Debit	Credit	Balance
1990					
June					

Date	Holt, H. Explanation	Post. Ref.	Debit	Credit	Balance
1990					
June					

Date	Mifflin, M. Explanation	Post. Ref.	Debit	Credit	Balance
1990					
June					

Date	Nobel, N. Explanation	Post. Ref.	Debit	Credit	Balance
1990					
June					

PROBLEM **B7-7**

Tom Finn Retail Store *(continued)*

Accounts Payable Subsidiary Ledger

Date		Action Inc. Explanation	Post. Ref.	Debit	Credit	Balance
1990						
June						

Date		Instant, Inc. Explanation	Post. Ref.	Debit	Credit	Balance
1990						
June						

Date		Swift Company Explanation	Post. Ref.	Debit	Credit	Balance
1990						
June						

Date		Timley, Ltd. Explanation	Post. Ref.	Debit	Credit	Balance
1990						
June						

PROBLEM **B7-7**

NAME
SECTION
DATE

Tom Finn Retail Store *(continued)*

7.

TOM FINN RETAIL STORE
Income Statement
Month Ended June 30, 1990

TOM FINN RETAIL STORE
Statement of Owner's Equity
Month Ended June 30, 1990

PROBLEM **B7-7**

Tom Finn Retail Store *(concluded)*

TOM FINN RETAIL STORE
Balance Sheet
June 30, 1990

Assets		Liabilities & Owner's Equity	

TOM FINN RETAIL STORE
Schedule of Accounts Receivable
June 30, 1990

Barnes, B.	
Mifflin, M.	
Nobel, N.	
Total	

TOM FINN RETAIL STORE
Schedule of Accounts Payable
June 30, 1990

Action Inc.	
Instant, Inc.	
Swift Company	
Total	

CHAPTER 7 DECISION PROBLEM

Mississippi Transport Company

NAME
SECTION
DATE

PROBLEM **B8-2**

Pawloski Real Estate

NAME
SECTION
DATE

1. PAWLOSKI REAL ESTATE Bank Reconciliation May 31, 1990		

2.	General Journal			
Date	Account Titles and Explanation	Post. Ref.	Debit	Credit
1990				

PROBLEM **B8-4**

Camp-Out Inc.

NAME

SECTION

DATE

1. Gross Method — **General Journal**

Date	Account Titles and Explanation	Post. Ref.	Debit	Credit
1991				

PROBLEM **B8-4**

Camp-Out Inc. *(continued)*

2. CAMP-OUT INC. Income Statement For Month Ended April 30, 1991		

3. Net method	General Journal			
Date	Account Titles and Explanation	Post. Ref.	Debit	Credit
1991				

PROBLEM **B8-4**

Camp-Out Inc. *(continued)*

NAME
SECTION
DATE

	General Journal			
		Post.		
Date	Account Titles and Explanation	Ref.	Debit	Credit
1991				

PROBLEM **B8-4**

Camp-Out Inc. *(concluded)*

4.

CAMP-OUT INC.
Income Statement
For Month Ended April 30, 1991

PROBLEM **B8-5**

Metro Rock Co. *(concluded)*

Voucher register for this problem is at the back of this book.

NAME

SECTION

DATE

METRO ROCK CO.
Check Register

Date	Check Number	Payee	Vou. No.	Vouchers Payable Debit	Purchase Discounts Credit	Cash Credit
1991						

General Journal

Date	Account Titles and Explanation	Post. Ref.	Debit	Credit
1991				

CHAPTER 8 DECISION PROBLEM

Interstate Wholesalers

MEMORANDUM

To:
From:
Re:

Interstate Wholesalers *(concluded)*

W. WIRGES PETTY CASH FUND Schedule Calculating Cash Missing		

Date		General Journal Account Titles and Explanation	Post. Ref.	Debit	Credit
1991					

PROBLEM **B9-2**

Rochester Wholesale Video

NAME
SECTION
DATE

PROBLEM **B9-3**

Brite Sound & Sight Co.

NAME
SECTION
DATE

1.

ACCOUNTS RECEIVABLE AGING SCHEDULE
September 30, 1990

Customer's Name	Not Yet Due	1–60 Days Past Due	61–90 Days Past Due	91–120 Days Past Due	Over 120 Days Past Due
Mosley Stereo					
Buckner Systems Inc.					
Stevens T.V.					
Spivey Sounds Co.					
Murphy Department Store					
Waters Appliances					
Ezelle T.V. & Stereo					
Jacob Stores					
Geiger Sales Co.					
Bidwell Hi-Fi					
Van Zant Stereo Town					
Hutson Speaker World					
Eller Stereo Inc.					
Cooke Boutique					
Parsons Electronics					
Moore Audio Inc.					
Knipe Sound Systems					
Pricher Bargain Center					
Totals					

PROBLEM **B9-3**

Brite Sound & Sight Co. *(concluded)*

Estimate of Uncollectible Accounts
September 30, 1990

Age Category	Amount in the Age Category	% Expected to Be Uncollectible	Amount Expected to Be Uncollectible
Not yet due			
1–60 days past due			
61–90 days past due			
91–120 days past due			
Over 120 days past due			
Total			

2.

General Journal

Date	Account Titles and Explanation	Post. Ref.	Debit	Credit
1990				
3.				

PROBLEM **B9-5**

Oliver Wire Co.

NAME
SECTION
DATE

1.

2.

Date		General Journal Account Titles and Explanation	Post. Ref.	Debit	Credit
1990					

PROBLEM **B9-6**

Chester Security

NAME

SECTION

DATE

1.

General Journal

Date		Account Titles and Explanation	Post. Ref.	Debit	Credit
1991					

2.

PROBLEM **B9-7**

Glacier's Men's Wear

NAME
SECTION
DATE

1.

General Journal

Date		Account Titles and Explanation	Post. Ref.	Debit	Credit
1991					

PROBLEM **B9-7**

Glacier's Men's Wear *(concluded)*

Date	Account Titles and Explanation	Post. Ref.	Debit	Credit
1991				
2.				

3. GLACIER'S MEN'S WEAR Partial Balance Sheet December 31, 1991		
Calculations:		

PROBLEM **B9-8**

Fairlane Products Inc.

NAME
SECTION
DATE

1. Name of Company's Stock Owned	Original Cost	Market Value Dec. 31, 1990
Biotech Research Co.		
Plains Machinery Inc.		
Interlakes Telephone Co.		
Automotive Electronics		
Total		

Calculation of cost and market value of each stock owned:

2.

General Journal

Date	Account Titles and Explanation	Post. Ref.	Debit	Credit
1990				
3.				

CHAPTER 9 DECISION PROBLEM

Encore Plumbing Wholesalers

NAME
SECTION
DATE

Date		General Journal	Post. Ref.	Debit	Credit

PROBLEM **B10-1**

Keeley Corp.

NAME
SECTION
DATE

Ending Inventory and Cost of Goods Sold Calculations

Weighted average ending inventory:

Weighted average cost of goods sold:

PROBLEM **B10-3**

Kathy's Kitchen World

NAME
SECTION
DATE

Description	(A) Inventory Stock No.	(B) Quantity	(C) Cost (FIFO)	(D) Market	(E) Item-by-Item LCM	
1. LCM ending inventory item-by-item basis (total of column E)						
2. LCM for inventory as a whole (smaller) of column C and column D totals)						

PROBLEM **B10-4**

Blue Powder Ski Shop

NAME
SECTION
DATE

PROBLEM **B10-5**

Cruise Casuals

NAME

SECTION

DATE

CRUISE CASUALS Calculation of Ending Inventory Using Retail Inventory Method May 31, 1990	Cost	Retail

PROBLEM **B10-6**

Betsy's Ceramic Supply

NAME

SECTION

DATE

1.

Calculation of Ending Inventory
Using Retail Inventory Method
June 30, 1990

		Cost	Retail

2.

BETSY'S CERAMIC SUPPLY
Income Statement
Period September 1, 1989–June 30, 1990

PROBLEM **B10-6**

Betsy's Ceramic Supply *(concluded)*

3.

BETSY'S CERAMIC SUPPLY
Balance Sheet
June 30, 1990

Assets

Liabilities & Owner's Equity

PROBLEM **B10-7**

Tacoma Inc.

NAME

SECTION

DATE

Calculation of Corrected Net Income for Each of 4 Years

Description	1988	1989	1990	1991
Net income reported	$60000	$ 35600	$18000	$(2000)
a. 1988 ending inventory understated; 1989 beginning inventory understated	12600	(12600)		

PROBLEM **B10-9**

Oregon Industries

Foldout working papers for problem B10-8 are at the back of this book.

NAME
SECTION
DATE

FIFO Perpetual Inventory:

Item: Paper Tape no. TP370

Date	PURCHASES			COST OF GOODS SOLD			INVENTORY ON HAND		
	Quantity	Unit Cost	Total Cost	Quantity	Unit Cost	Total Cost	Quantity	Unit Cost	Total Cost

PROBLEM **B10-9**

Oregon Industries *(continued)*

LIFO Perpetual Inventory:

Item: Paper Tape no. TP370

Date	PURCHASES			COST OF GOODS SOLD			INVENTORY ON HAND		
	Quantity	Unit Cost	Total Cost	Quantity	Unit Cost	Total Cost	Quantity	Unit Cost	Total Cost

PROBLEM **B10-9**

Oregon Industries *(concluded)*

NAME

SECTION

DATE

FIFO ending inventory:

FIFO cost of goods sold:

LIFO ending inventory:

LIFO cost of goods sold:

NAME

SECTION

DATE

CHAPTER 10 DECISION PROBLEM

Arrowhead Optics

1.

Income Statements	FIFO	Weighted Average	LIFO

Ending inventory calculations:

2.

3.

PROBLEM **B11-2**

Eager Industries

NAME
SECTION
DATE

1. Straight-line depreciation:

2. Units-of-output depreciation:

3. Sum-of-the-years'-digits depreciation:

PROBLEM **B11-2**

Eager Industries *(concluded)*

4. Double declining-balance depreciation:

Depreciation rate $= 2(\frac{1}{6}) = \frac{2}{6} = \frac{1}{3}$, or .33333

Year	Asset Cost	− Accumulated Depreciation Jan. 1	= Book Value Jan. 1	Depreciation Rate	Double Declining-Balance Depreciation Expense
1989	$64000				
1990	64000				
1991	64000				
1992	64000				
1993	64000				
1994	64000				

PROBLEM **B11-3**

Blackwelder Inc.

NAME

SECTION

DATE

Office furniture — double declining-balance depreciation:

Telephone system — straight-line depreciation:

Building — Sum-of-the-years'-digits depreciation:

PROBLEM **B11-4**

Marine Transport

NAME

SECTION

DATE

General Journal

Date		Account Titles and Explanation	Post. Ref.	Debit	Credit

PROBLEM **B11-4**

Marine Transport *(concluded)*

PROPERTY, PLANT, AND EQUIPMENT SUBSIDIARY LEDGER RECORD

Asset: ______________________ **General Ledger Account:** ______________________

Identification No.: ______________________ **Mfg. Serial No.:** ______________________

Location: ______________________

Acquired from: ______________________ **Brand:** ______________________

Responsible Person: ______________________

Est. Life: ____________ **Salvage Value:** ____________ **Depr. Method:** ____________

Depr. Per Year: ____________ **Depr. Per Month:** ____________

Date	P/R	Asset			Accumulated Depreciation			Book Value
		Debit	Credit	Balance	Debit	Credit	Balance	

PROBLEM **B11-6**

Tryon Airlines

NAME
SECTION
DATE

		General Journal			
			Post.		
Date		Account Titles and Explanation	Ref.	Debit	Credit
1990					

PROBLEM **B11-6**

Tryon Airlines *(concluded)*

	General Journal			
Date	**Account Titles and Explanation**	**Post. Ref.**	**Debit**	**Credit**
1990				

PROBLEM **B11-7**

Elite Moving

NAME

SECTION

DATE

	General Journal			
		Post.		
Date	Account Titles and Explanation	Ref.	Debit	Credit
1990				

PROBLEM **B11-7**

Elite Moving *(concluded)*

Date	General Journal Account Titles and Explanation	Post. Ref.	Debit	Credit
1991				

PROBLEM **B11-8**

Discovery Enterprises

NAME
SECTION
DATE

1.	General Journal			
		Post.		
Date	Account Titles and Explanation	Ref.	Debit	Credit
1990				
2.				

CHAPTER 11 DECISION PROBLEM

Jason's and Angela's Donuts

NAME

SECTION

DATE

Jason's and Angela's Donuts *(concluded)*

PROBLEM **B12-1**

Denver Drilling Company

NAME
SECTION
DATE

1.

DENVER DRILLING COMPANY
Computation of Take-Home Pay
Week Ending February 9, 1990

	East	North	South	Total
Gross earnings:				
Regular hours				
Overtime hours				
Total earnings				
Deductions:				
Federal income taxes				
FICA taxes				
Union dues				
Total deductions				
Net pay				

2.

General Journal

Date		Account Titles and Explanation	Post. Ref.	Debit	Credit
1990					
Feb.	9				

PROBLEM **B12-2**

Dauntless Company

NAME

SECTION

DATE

Date		General Journal Account Titles and Explanation	Post. Ref.	Debit	Credit
1990					
Oct.					

PROBLEM **B12-3**

Voucher register for this problem is at the back of this book.

NAME
SECTION
DATE

New York Cement Company *(concluded)*

		NEW YORK CEMENT COMPANY Check Register				
Date	**Check Number**	**Payee**	**Vouch. No.**	**Vouchers Payable Debit**	**Purchases Discount Credit**	**Cash Credit**
Nov.						

	General Journal			
Date	**Account Titles and Explanation**	**Post. Ref.**	**Debit**	**Credit**
1990				
Nov.				

PROBLEM **B12-4**

Dallas Consulting Company

NAME
SECTION
DATE

1.

DALLAS CONSULTING COMPANY
Payroll Register
For the Week Ended November 23, 1990

Employee	Total Hours	Earnings			Taxable Earnings	
		Regular	Overtime	Total	FICA	Unemployment Compensation
Adams, Zeke						
Baker, Yvonne						
Clark, Xello						
Dunn, William						
Eastman, Varney						
Fair, Uris						

Deductions						Payment		Distribution	
FIT	FICA	Union Dues	Health Insurance	U.S. Savings Bonds	Total	Net Pay	Check No.	Office Salaries	Warehouse Salaries

PROBLEM **B12-4**

Dallas Consulting Company *(concluded)*

2.	General Journal			
Date	Account Titles and Explanation	Post. Ref.	Debit	Credit
1990				
Nov.				

PROBLEM **B12-5**

Nancy Reagins

NAME
SECTION
DATE

1. and **2.**

NAME	Reagins, Nancy	TELEPHONE	(404) 432-1376	SOCIAL SECURITY NUMBER	242-21-5788
ADDRESS	2731 Roswell Road Roswell, Georgia 30067	DATE EMPLOYED	Oct. 18, 1975	DATE OF BIRTH	May 15, 1955
DATE TERMINATED		REASON			
MARRIED	(XX)				
SINGLE	( )	PAY RATE	$17,000		
HEAD OF HOUSEHOLD	( )	HOURLY PAY	$8.50		
DEPARTMENT	Production				

1990 Period Ending	Earnings: Total Hours	Regular Hours	Overtime Hours	Total	Cumulative	Deductions: FIT	FICA	Union Dues	Health Ins.	U.S. Bonds	Total	Net Pay	Check No.
Jan. 12	80	680.00		680.00	680.00	55.00	51.00	7.00	9.15		122.15	557.85	315
26	88	680.00	102.00	782.00	1,462.00	70.00	59.40	7.00	9.15		145.55	636.45	487
Feb. 9	80	680.00		680.00	2,142.00	55.00	51.00	7.00	9.15		122.15	577.85	608
23	80	680.00		680.00	2,822.00	55.00	51.00	7.00	9.15		122.15	577.85	756
Mar. 9	80	680.00		680.00	3,502.00	55.00	51.00	7.00	9.15		122.15	577.85	821
23													
1st QTR.													

PROBLEM **B12-6**

Clairmont Company

NAME
SECTION
DATE

General Journal

Date		Account Titles and Explanation	Post. Ref.	Debit	Credit
1989					
Jan.					
Feb.					
Apr.					
May					
July					
Nov.					

PROBLEM **B12-6**

Clairmont Company *(concluded)*

General Journal					
Date		**Account Titles and Explanation**	**Post. Ref.**	**Debit**	**Credit**
1989					
Dec.					
1990					
Jan.	30				

PROBLEM **B12-7**

Ajax Company

NAME
SECTION
DATE

Date		General Journal Account Titles and Explanation	Post. Ref.	Debit	Credit
1989					
Jan.	1				
to					
June	30				
July	1				
to					
Dec.	31				
Dec.	31				
Jan.	1				
to					
June	30				

NAME
SECTION
DATE

Analysis of Income from Realty Sales

If 20 individuals are employed:

If 20 agents are engaged:

PROBLEM **B13-1**

NAME
SECTION
DATE

Barthles and Jaynes Storage and Sales

1.

General Journal				
Date	Account Titles and Explanation	Post. Ref.	Debit	Credit

2.

Statement of Partners' Capital Accounts For the 6 Months Ended December 31, 1989	Barthles	Jaynes	Total

PROBLEM **B13-2**

Dewey, Soakum, and Howe

NAME
SECTION
DATE

Computation of Profit Distribution

	Dewey	Soakum	Howe	Total
1.				
2.				
3.				
4.				

PROBLEM **B13-4**

Kirby and Stickney

NAME

SECTION

DATE

Date		General Journal Account Titles and Explanation	Post. Ref.	Debit	Credit
1.					
2.					

PROBLEM **B13-5**

Dizzy Video Store

NAME
SECTION
DATE

1.

DIZZY VIDEO STORE Income Statement Year Ended December 31, 1989		

2.

DIZZY VIDEO STORE Statement of Partners' Capital Accounts Year Ended December 31, 1989				
	Hewey	Dewey	Lewey	Totals

PROBLEM **B13-5**

Dizzy Video Store *(concluded)*

3.

DIZZY VIDEO STORE
Balance Sheet
December 31, 1989

Assets		Liabilities and Partners' Equity	

PROBLEM **B13-6**

Carnac Enterprises

NAME
SECTION
DATE

Date	General Journal Account Titles and Explanation	Post. Ref.	Debit	Credit
1.				
2.				
3.				
4.				

PROBLEM **B13-7**

NAME
SECTION
DATE

Jackson, Cipriano, and Ackerman

General Journal

Date	Account Titles and Explanation	Post. Ref.	Debit	Credit

PROBLEM **B13-8**

Larry, Darryl, and Bob

NAME
SECTION
DATE

1.

LARRY, DARRYL, AND BOB
Partnership Liquidation Schedule

	Cash	+	Other Assets	=	Accounts Payable	+	Larry, Capital	+	Darryl, Capital	+	Bob, Capital

2.

LARRY, DARRYL, AND BOB
Partnership Liquidation Schedule

	Cash	+	Other Assets	=	Accounts Payable	+	Larry, Capital	+	Darryl, Capital	+	Bob, Capital

PROBLEM **B13-8**

Larry, Darryl, and Bob *(concluded)*

3.

LARRY, DARRYL, AND BOB
Partnership Liquidation Schedule

	Cash	+	Other Assets	=	Accounts Payable	+	Larry, Capital	+	Darryl, Capital	+	Bob, Capital

PROBLEM **B13-9**

Larry, Darryl, and Bob

NAME
SECTION
DATE

1.

LARRY, DARRYL, AND BOB
Partnership Liquidation Schedule

	Cash	+	Other Assets	=	Accounts Payable	+	Larry, Capital	+	Darryl, Capital	+	Bob, Capital

2.

LARRY, DARRYL, AND BOB
Partnership Liquidation Schedule

	Cash	+	Other Assets	=	Accounts Payable	+	Larry, Capital	+	Darryl, Capital	+	Bob, Capital

PROBLEM **B13-9**

Larry, Darryl, and Bob *(concluded)*

3.

LARRY, DARRYL, AND BOB
Partnership Liquidation Schedule

	Cash	+	Other Assets	=	Accounts Payable	+	Larry, Capital	+	Darryl, Capital	+	Bob, Capital

CHAPTER 13 DECISION PROBLEM

NAME

SECTION

DATE

Bill, Jack, and Bob

	Profit Distribution Schedule			
	25%	30%	45%	
	Bill	Jack	Bob	Total
	Bill	Jack	Bob	Total
	Bill	Jack	Bob	Total

Bill, Jack, and Bob *(concluded)*

PROBLEM **B14-1**

Classic Corp.

NAME
SECTION
DATE

		General Journal			
Date		**Account Titles and Explanation**	**Post. Ref.**	**Debit**	**Credit**
1990					

PROBLEM **B14-2**

NAME
SECTION
DATE

Blanco Inc.

	General Journal			
Date	Account Titles and Explanation	Post. Ref.	Debit	Credit
1989				

PROBLEM **B14-3**

Coyote Enterprises Inc.

NAME
SECTION
DATE

	General Journal			
Date	**Account Titles and Explanation**	**Post. Ref.**	**Debit**	**Credit**
1991				

PROBLEM **B14-4**

Rampart Inc.

NAME
SECTION
DATE

1.	**Preferred**	**Common**	**Total**

2.	**Preferred**	**Common**	**Total**

PROBLEM **B14-4**

Rampart Inc. *(concluded)*

3.	Preferred	Common	Total

PROBLEM **B14-5**

Toney Company

NAME
SECTION
DATE

1.

Cash

Land

Preferred Stock

Common Stock

Stock Subscriptions Receivable

Organization Costs

Paid-In Capital in Excess of Par: Preferred

Common Stock Subscribed

PROBLEM **B14-5**

Toney Company *(continued)*

Paid-In Capital in Excess of Par: Common

Paid-In Capital from Treasury Stock

Donated Capital

Treasury Stock

Retained Earnings

PROBLEM **B14-5**

NAME
SECTION
DATE

Toney Company *(concluded)*

2.

TONEY COMPANY
Stockholders' Equity
December 31, 1990

PROBLEM **B14-6**

Goodeal Inc.

NAME

SECTION

DATE

GOODEAL INC. Stockholders' Equity December 31, 1991		

NAME

SECTION

DATE

CHAPTER 14 DECISION PROBLEM

H & D Corp.

1.

2.

3.

4.

5.

6.

7.

8.